D0429581

Do You Know
You're **Already**
Amazing?

Other Works by Holley Gerth

You're Already Amazing

You're Already Amazing LifeGrowth Guide

You're Already Amazing LifeGrowth DVD

You're Made for a God-Sized Dream

Opening the Door to Your God-Sized Dreams

You're Going to Be Okay

What Your Heart Needs for the Hard Days

You're Loved No Matter What

Do You Know You're **Already** Amazing?

30 TRUTHS TO SET YOUR HEART FREE

Holley Gerth

Revell

a division of Baker Publishing Group
Grand Rapids, Michigan

© 2016 by Holley, Inc.

Published by Revell
a division of Baker Publishing Group
P.O. Box 6287, Grand Rapids, MI 49516-6287
www.revellbooks.com

Printed in the United States of America

Library of Congress Cataloging-in-Publication Data
Names: Gerth, Holley, author. | Gerth, Holley. You're already amazing.
Title: Do you know you're already amazing? : 30 truths to set your heart free
    / Holley Gerth.
Description: Grand Rapids, MI : Revell, a division of Baker Publishing
    Group, [2017] | Devotional based on author's You're already amazing. |
    Includes bibliographical references.
Identifiers: LCCN 2016013494 | ISBN 9780800726973 (cloth)
Subjects: LCSH: Christian women—Religious life—Meditations. | Self-
    acceptance in women—Religious aspects—Christianity—Meditations.
Classification: LCC BV4527 .G4655 2012 | DDC 248.8/43—dc23
LC record available at https://lccn.loc.gov/2016013494

In keeping with biblical principles of creation stewardship, Baker Publishing Group advocates the responsible use of our natural resources. As a member of the Green Press Initiative, our company uses recycled paper when possible. The text paper of this book is composed in part of post-consumer waste.

green
press
INITIATIVE

16 17 18 19 20 21 22   7 6 5 4 3 2 1

I praise you because *you made me* in an *amazing* and wonderful way.

Psalm 139:14 NCV

To my grandma, *Eula,*

my mom, *Lynda,*

and my daughter, *Lovelle* —

your love helps me believe the

truth about who I am.

Contents

Why We Need to Know the Truth about Who We Are

I pose this question to a group of women online one evening: "What lies are our hearts tempted to believe? Think about yourself but also your daughters, sisters, friends, and others." I expect a trickle of responses, but instead I'm struck by a waterfall of words. Hundreds of women share confessions like, "I'm inadequate," "I feel invisible," and "If anyone really knew me, they wouldn't love me the same way."

I nod in understanding and feel a fierce longing to reach through my computer screen and wrap protective arms around every person who has left a comment.

Our battle against the lies our hearts believe goes all the way back to Eden. The enemy tempted Eve with the question, "Did God really say . . . ?" That phrase is the tip on every sword of untruth. And he still uses it to pierce the deepest parts of who we are.

Did God really say you're loved?

Did God really say you're enough?

Did God really say he has a good plan for your life?

Before we know it, the lies slip in and our joy, peace, and sense of purpose slip out. But we don't have to live that way. We belong to a Savior who promised, "You will know the truth, and the truth will set you free" (John 8:32). How do we discover this truth? Through an intimate relationship with Jesus, the One who is "the way and the truth and the life" (John 14:6). Here's the secret: Truth is not just a fact we store in our heads. *Truth is a Person we seek with our hearts*. We do so by spending intentional time with him and hearing what he has to say.

More than one hundred thousand women have read *You're Already Amazing* (the book this devotional is based on). I addressed the lies we believe in one chapter, and readers told me, "We want more!" This devotional goes far beyond that original content, which covered only five lies, and instead addresses thirty. It includes powerful Scriptures, new insights, and prayer prompts to help you draw close to Jesus and receive the truth he wants to whisper to your heart. When you finish, you'll also be better equipped to share encouraging truth with other women in your life who need to hear it too.

Psalm 139:14 declares, "I praise you because you made me in an amazing and wonderful way" (NCV). In other words, recognizing the truth about who we are leads to *praise*, not to pride. Honoring our Maker is the ultimate goal of what we're doing together.

We may have been wounded by lies, but we have not lost the battle. And we have been promised victory. We're going to defeat discouragement, banish fear, and break free from all that's been keeping us from embracing who we are and becoming all God created us to be.

It's time for us to fight until we fully believe the truth about who we are, because we bring

God glory and change the world when we do. (If that still sounds a bit wild and scandalous to you, just keep reading. I used to feel that way too.)

Let's win this war for our hearts together, sisters.

Are you with me?

Why We Need to Know the Truth about Who We Are

About This Devotional

Each of the thirty devotions in this book addresses a lie our hearts are tempted to believe and shares the truth God wants to offer us instead.

The truths and lies shared are based on actual conversations I've had with women as an author, blogger, counselor, speaker, and life coach. While each day's reading has a woman's name connected with it to make it feel more personal, for privacy reasons these are not the actual names of any particular people. Instead they're examples based on real instances that are intended to provide stories and perspectives we can all relate to. I've also included women from the Bible because they struggled with lies just as we do now. Sometimes what they say is quoted directly from

Scripture, and sometimes I've paraphrased the truths their stories tell us.

Following each devotional entry are prayer prompts. While the messages provide truth that applies to all of us, it's important to spend time with Jesus sharing the specific lies you've believed and asking him to reveal the truth you especially need to hear. If he seems silent, that's totally okay too. Just enjoy some peaceful moments being with him as you would with someone you love.

While you'll have peaceful moments, confronting the lies we believe really is doing battle. If you struggle with insecurity or other challenging emotions at times as you go through this book, know that's normal. Keep fighting, and ask God to guard your heart. You can't lose with him on your side! It can also be really helpful to share your thoughts with someone you trust and ask for extra prayer. The more we get honest about the lies we hear, the more we help each other heal.

Life can be busy, and you'll probably miss days at some point. If so, just pick up where you left off and continue. Give yourself grace on this journey,

About This Devotional

and treat yourself with extra gentleness. Try to avoid attacking yourself with critical thoughts or unrealistic expectations. Instead stay focused on what matters most—and that's simply connecting with Jesus, who always welcomes you.

Also remember that it takes time for what we know is true to actually *feel* true. If your emotions and experiences don't change right away, just keep repeating the truth to yourself day after day. Our brains create new neural pathways when we begin thinking differently, and that's not an instant event but a process. As you persevere you'll be "transformed by the renewing of your mind" (Rom. 12:2), and your emotions will eventually catch up.

Sharing what we're learning with others can strengthen our minds as well as our hearts and speed up the change process. Consider inviting someone in your life or even a group of women to go through this book with you. You can do a thirty-one-day truth challenge together! Be creative—you can meet in person, set up a group online, talk on the phone, or whatever works best for you.

I hope it will feel like I'm joining in with you too! I'm excited about what our God of Truth is going to speak to you and the new victories he's going to bring in your life. *He loves you even more than you know right now.* "I pray that you, being rooted and established in love, may have power, together with all the Lord's holy people, to grasp how wide and long and high and deep is the love of Christ, and to know this love that surpasses knowledge—that you may be filled to the measure of all the fullness of God" (Eph. 3:17–19).

1

You're Not Invisible

The lie we hear: "I'm invisible."—Emma

The truth our hearts need: "God sees me."
—Hagar

Read Genesis 16

Emma groans as she sees the mountain of laundry in front of her. She takes the first load to the washer, and her thoughts begin swirling just like the water inside. The day has begun much like any other. Juice spilled. Homework lost, then found. Car doors slammed. Does anyone even appreciate what she does?

She thinks back to her internship during college. She made coffee, took notes in meetings, and answered to a boss who couldn't be pleased. One evening she found herself alone in the dark when the janitor flipped off the lights. An unfinished report still sat on her desk, and she quietly whispered, "I just want someone to notice what I do."

She wonders if it will be the same in her later years of life too. She pictures herself wandering around a now-empty house. Maybe the phone will ring sometimes. Hopefully, she'll have friends and family who will come to visit. But will anyone really value her when she isn't as useful?

Emma pauses, and the lie she's fought many times in life drifts to the surface of her mind: *I'm invisible.*

If Hagar could have heard Emma's thoughts, she would have nodded in understanding. Although she lived thousands of years ago, her duties also included lots of work and little appreciation. And as a servant to Sarai (later called

Do You Know You're Already Amazing?

Sarah), the wife of Abraham, Hagar also had to do something that would be totally unacceptable in our culture: have a child for her boss. God had promised Sarai and Abraham a son. When it didn't happen in the time frame Sarai hoped, she bypassed God's plan and turned to Hagar for a solution.

But rather than providing peace for Sarai, Hagar's pregnancy led to even more tension in the household. Finally Hagar fled to the desert out of desperation. She must have felt alone, overlooked, and deeply concerned for her unborn child. No one understood all she'd been through and what she'd had to do. Who would look out for her now? Then an angel appeared to Hagar and spoke words of hope and encouragement. Hagar "gave this name to the LORD who spoke to her: 'You are the God who sees me,' for she said, 'I have now seen the One who sees me'" (Gen. 16:13).

Sometimes our lives can feel like we're in the middle of a desert alone. The work we have to do seems as abundant as the sand. We're thirsty for affirmation and a little recognition. Feelings of being overlooked and unappreciated pile up

You're Not Invisible

like dunes (or piles of laundry) in our souls. We wonder if our lives even matter. Yet in those overlooked places, God comes to us and whispers, "*I see you. I* know your past, present, and future. There will never be a moment when I'm not watching over you."

Emma grabs a pair of jeans to add to the washer, and a slip of paper drifts to the floor. One of the kids must have carried it home from church yesterday. She rolls her eyes and thinks, "Great, one more thing I have to pick up today." Then the Scripture at the top captures her attention:

> O LORD, you have examined my heart
> and know everything about me.
> You know when I sit down or stand up.
> You know my thoughts even when I'm
> far away.
> You see me when I travel
> and when I rest at home.
> You know everything I do.
>
> Psalm 139:1–3 NLT

Suddenly the laundry room feels like sacred ground. *Perhaps it always has been,* Emma re-

Do You Know You're Already Amazing?

alizes. She senses the loving gaze of the God who spoke the stars into being, sculpted the sand, and numbers the hairs on her head. The washer stills and her anxious thoughts finally do as well. Even if no one else ever sees all she does, God notices and cares. He is with her in all the ordinary, extraordinary moments. He always has been. He always will be. And one day after she's finished serving faithfully, she'll stand before him—as we all will—to say as Hagar did, "I have now seen the One who sees me."

Truth Your Heart Needs

Talk with God about the lies you battle, and ask him to reveal what's true. Listen for his loving voice in your heart, look to his Word, and be honest about what you're feeling.

◆ **What's a Lie I've Battled?** (Example: *I'm invisible.*)

◆ **When or How Did I Begin Battling This Lie?** Ask God to bring a specific memory to mind. If one doesn't come, that's totally okay. Just leave this blank.

Do You Know You're Already Amazing?

◆ **How Do I Need to Be Healed from the Ways This Lie Has Wounded Me?** Write a prayer sharing honestly with God about how this lie has hurt you and asking him to heal your heart.

◆ **What's the Truth That Will Defeat This Lie in My Life?** (Example: *God sees me.*) Ask God what's really true, and take time to listen for his answer. It may come from today's Scriptures, the devotional, encouraging words from someone in your life, or his still small voice within your heart.

◆ **Tip:** If you'd like help finding additional Scriptures for this section each day, you can use a site like BibleGateway.com. Just enter a keyword in the search box, and it will give you a list of related verses.

2

You're Not Forgotten

"God has forgotten me."—Maria

"God remembers me."—Hannah

Read 1 Samuel 1:1–2:11

Maria fights back tears and forces a smile as her friend announces, "I'm engaged!" She thinks of the row of oddly colored bridesmaid dresses hanging in her closet and wonders if she'll have room for another. "I'd much rather put a husband's clothes in that spot, Lord," she silently protests.

"Why are you answering everyone's prayers but mine? Have you forgotten me? I must have done something to upset you or I'd be married by now."

Scenarios like this one have been repeated throughout human history. Our hearts have an unmet desire like being married, having a baby, getting a promotion, or another dream. Then we watch as God says yes to those around us but seems to overlook what we want.

Hannah knew that kind of pain intimately. She longed for children, and yet her arms remained empty. In her culture, not having children was a source of deep shame, and barrenness was seen as divine punishment. Society (not God) even allowed a husband to take a second wife in order to produce children. It appears that's what happened in Hannah's case. And the second spouse was a first-rate pain. "Whenever Hannah went up to the house of the LORD, her rival provoked her till she wept and would not eat" (1 Sam. 1:6). Hannah arrived at the temple so distraught that Eli the priest assumed she must be drunk. When she explained the true source of her distress, he encouraged her and prayed for God to grant her request. The child she became pregnant with soon after grew up to be Samuel, one of the greatest prophets to ever serve Israel.

Scripture says about Hannah, "The LORD remembered her" (1 Sam. 1:19). At first I was taken aback by those words. Surely God hadn't ever forgotten Hannah or her request! When I looked deeper into the Hebrew meaning of the word, I discovered it more specifically means looking on someone with kindness and granting a request. We can feel forgotten too when it seems God isn't answering our prayers. But God is always aware of every detail of our lives.

> But Zion said, "The LORD has forsaken
>   me,
>   the Lord has forgotten me."
> [Then God answers,]
>   "Can a mother forget the baby at her
>   breast
>   and have no compassion on the child
>   she has borne?
> Though she may forget,
>   I will not forget you!"
>
>   Isaiah 49:14–15

Do You Know You're Already Amazing?

I personally went through a season of feeling similar to Maria and Hannah when my husband and I struggled with infertility for almost a decade. We faced grief, losses, and hard questions that didn't seem to have answers. Several years into our journey, God placed a dream in our hearts to one day adopt an older child who'd had a difficult background or aged out of the foster system. We thought it would be later in our lives, but he recently brought our daughter, Lovelle, to us when she was twenty.

As I saw God's care and provisions in every detail of our story with Lovelle, I realized this: it wasn't that I had done something *wrong*; it was that the timing for God to give us a daughter hadn't yet been *right*. Do I fully understand God's mysterious journey for our lives? No, and I don't think I will until I get to heaven. But Lovelle and I often say to each other now, "I would go through it all again to get to you!" I imagine Hannah would have said the same to Samuel. And Maria will too when she meets the man God has for her.

We have not been forgotten. God isn't ignoring our needs or waiting for us to be perfect before he answers our prayers. Instead he's working out his plans for us long before we ever catch a glimpse of what he's doing. "Faith is confidence in what we hope for and assurance about what we do not see" (Heb. 11:1). That kind of soul-sustaining belief comes not from what we're hoping *for* but from who we're placing our hope *in*. Our God is good and he loves us. Even when we can't see his hands, we can still trust his heart.

Truth Your Heart Needs

Talk with God about the lies you battle, and ask him to reveal what's true. Listen for his loving voice in your heart, look to his Word, and be honest about what you're feeling.

◆ **What's a Lie I've Battled?** (Example: *God has forgotten me.*)

◆ **When or How Did I Begin Battling This Lie?** Ask God to bring a specific memory to mind. If one doesn't come, that's totally okay. Just leave this blank.

◆ **How Do I Need to Be Healed from the Ways This Lie Has Wounded Me?** Write a prayer sharing honestly with God about how this lie has hurt you and asking him to heal your heart.

◆ **What's the Truth That Will Defeat This Lie in My Life?** (Example: *God remembers me.*) Ask God what's really true, and take time to listen for his answer. It may come from today's Scriptures, the devotional, encouraging words from someone in your life, or his still small voice within your heart.

3

You Don't Need to Do It All

"I need to do it all."—Martha

"I only need to give Jesus my all."—Mary

Read Luke 10:38–42

Martha looks at the dirty dishes scattered across the counter and shakes her head. The smell of something burning prompts her to rescue the bread just in time. She notices a dust bunny hiding in the corner and quickly swats at it in hopes it will drift out of sight. What a busy day! *Where is my sister?*

In the other room she can hear the quiet murmur of voices. Jesus and his disciples have honored her home with a visit, and she wants to be sure everything is just right. For as long as Martha can remember, this has been her role. She's the responsible one who gets things done.

A feminine voice drifts her way from the conversation, and she can hardly believe her ears. Is that Mary? She leans around the doorway and sees her sister sitting at the feet of Jesus. The bag of items Martha sent her to get from the market hours ago is still by her side. It's yet another frustration in a long, hectic day, and Martha finally snaps. "Lord, don't you care that my sister has left me to do the work by myself? Tell her to help me!" (Luke 10:40).

I can so relate to the first phrase Martha utters: "Lord, don't you care?" It gives us such insight into her heart, into *our* hearts. So many times we believe "I need to do it all," because if we can, then surely *someone will care*. We will be loved. We will be noticed. We will be affirmed.

Do You Know You're Already Amazing?

And maybe the restlessness deep inside will subside.

I hear deep compassion and a tender invitation in Jesus' response. "'Martha, Martha,' the Lord answered, 'you are worried and upset about many things, but few things are needed—or indeed only one. Mary has chosen what is better, and it will not be taken away from her'" (Luke 10:41–42).

Jesus acknowledges Martha's feelings: "You are worried and upset."

Then he releases her from her endless to-do list: "Few things are needed—or indeed only one."

And he closes with a cure for Martha's insecurity: "Mary has chosen what is better, and *it will not be taken away from her.*" Isn't so much of our striving so that something won't be taken from us? Affection, reputation, relationships, roles, or affirmation. Jesus subtly reminds Martha that only he can offer the security her heart longs for most. And she doesn't even have to earn it. Joanna Weaver says in *Having a Mary Heart in a Martha World,*

Just as he welcomed Mary to sit at his feet in the living room, just as he invited Martha to leave the kitchen for a while and share in the Better Part, Jesus bids us to come. In obedience to his invitation, we find the key to our longings, the secret to living beyond the daily pressures that would otherwise tear us apart. For as we learn what it means to choose the Better Part of intimacy with Christ, we begin to be changed.[1]

This world will wear us out. The enemy of our souls would love to see us distracted by anything "good" that's not God's best. The people around us will always have expectations and demands. It's up to us to make a different, better choice. Scripture says, "I can do all things through Christ who strengthens me" (Phil. 4:13 NKJV). But it never says we have to do it all. The God who created the world in seven days doesn't have any trouble with his to-do list. He didn't "hire" you like an employee to get work done. Instead he called you into a relationship of love.

Both Mary and Martha served Jesus. But on this day only Mary *enjoyed* him. When what we're doing for God causes us to be "worried

Do You Know You're Already Amazing?

and upset" like Martha, then we've drifted away from what God wants most from us. As the Westminster Shorter Catechism says, "Man's chief end is to glorify God, and to enjoy him forever." This story isn't really about the specific actions of these two women; it's about the attitudes behind their choices. Even our work can be an act of worship. That means the solution to the pressure we feel to "do it all" isn't simply doing less. Instead it's grasping even *more* how much we're already loved. That's what keeps our hearts at the feet of Jesus wherever we are, whatever he may ask us to do.

Truth Your Heart Needs

Talk with God about the lies you battle and ask him to reveal what's true. Listen for his loving voice in your heart, look to his Word, and be honest about what you're feeling.

◆ **What's a Lie I've Battled?** (Example: *I need to do it all.*)

◆ **When or How Did I Begin Battling This Lie?** Ask God to bring a specific memory to mind. If one doesn't come, that's totally okay. Just leave this blank.

Do You Know You're Already Amazing?

◆ **How Do I Need to Be Healed from the Ways This Lie Has Wounded Me?** Write a prayer sharing honestly with God about how this lie has hurt you and asking him to heal your heart.

◆ **What's the Truth That Will Defeat This Lie in My Life?** (Example: *I only need to give Jesus my all.*) Ask God what's really true, and take time to listen for his answer. It may come from today's Scriptures, the devotional, encouraging words from someone in your life, or his still small voice within your heart.

4

You're Not Defined by a Man

"The men in my life define me."—Evelyn

"God determines my identity and destiny."—Abigail

Read 1 Samuel 25:2-42

Evelyn covers her ears at the sound of raised voices in the living room. When the front door slams, she runs to the window and watches her dad drive away for good. "I must not be lovable enough," her childhood mind believes.

A few years later Evelyn finds herself climbing into a car rather than watching one drive away. "Come on," her date whispers into her ear. "If you really want to be with me, you can prove it." Afraid of being abandoned again, Evelyn complies, but when the guy never calls again, her self-worth takes another hit.

When she walks down the aisle, Evelyn is sure this time her heart won't be broken. Someone will finally make her feel safe and cherished forever. But every time her husband comes home late from work, the old fear creeps in again.

Beth Moore says in her book *So Long, Insecurity*, "Nothing is more baffling than our attempt to derive our womanhood from our men. We use guys like mirrors to see if we're valuable. Beautiful. Desirable. Worthy of Notice. Viable."[1] But only God can show us who we really are and fill the longing for love inside us.

If Abigail had met Evelyn, she surely would have sympathized with the temptation to find her worth through a man's eyes. Scripture describes

Abigail as "an intelligent and beautiful woman," but her husband Nabal was "surly and mean" (1 Sam. 25:3). Unlike Evelyn, Abigail probably didn't have a choice about the man in her life because her marriage was likely arranged. But she did have a choice about whether or not a man defined her identity and destiny. And one day that became a matter of life or death.

Before he officially became king of Israel, David wandered the countryside to escape being killed by Saul (the current king). A natural leader, David quickly gained hundreds of followers. David and his men made sure all the flocks on the land where they stayed remained safe. In return he would sometimes ask for provisions from their owners, which was customary during that time. Any reasonable person would respond favorably to the request, not only because of social expectations but also because it was known that David would one day be king. Yet when David's men approached Nabal, he offered only sarcasm and disrespect.

A servant alerted Abigail to the situation, and she "acted quickly" but "did not tell her husband

Nabal" (1 Sam. 25:18–19). She presented David and his men with a generous gift of provisions and also soothed the conflict with her words. She explained the questionable character of her husband. Then she turned the conversation with a powerful phrase: "As for me . . ." (1 Sam. 25:25). In other words, Abigail was clearly expressing, *I am not defined by the man in my life*. In a culture where a woman's identity was determined by her marriage, this was a bold proclamation.

It seems Abigail could make this declaration because she knew God intimately. She mentioned "the LORD" seven times in her brief speech to David. She ended by asking David to remember her when God gave him success. David responded, "Praise be to the LORD, the God of Israel, who has sent you today to meet me. May you be blessed for your good judgment and for keeping me from bloodshed this day" (1 Sam. 25:32). David valued Abigail's faith, character, and positive influence. In contrast, when Abigail returned home and told Nabal what she'd done, his wicked heart literally couldn't take it. When David heard the news that Abigail was

now a widow, he did more than remember her—
he asked her to be his wife.

Because Abigail refused to let a man define her identity, she opened the door for God to determine her destiny. And here's the hope in her story for Evelyn and all of us: we may have been hurt by men in the past, but our future includes a King who recognizes our true worth and invites us to be his forever.

Truth Your Heart Needs

Talk with God about the lies you battle, and ask him to reveal what's true. Listen for his loving voice in your heart, look to his Word, and be honest about what you're feeling.

◆ **What's a Lie I've Battled?** (Example: *The men in my life define me.*)

◆ **When or How Did I Begin Battling This Lie?** Ask God to bring a specific memory to mind. If one doesn't come, that's totally okay. Just leave this blank.

- **How Do I Need to Be Healed from the Ways This Lie Has Wounded Me?** Write a prayer sharing honestly with God about how this lie has hurt you and asking him to heal your heart.

- **What's the Truth That Will Defeat This Lie in My Life?** (Example: *God determines my identity and destiny.*) Ask God what's really true, and take time to listen for his answer. It may come from today's Scriptures, the devotional, encouraging words from someone in your life, or his still small voice within your heart.

5

Your Life Has a Purpose

"My life doesn't have a purpose."—Olivia

"I'm here for such a time as this."—Esther

Read Esther 4

Olivia drums the edge of her pen against the table to a rhythm that matches the questions marching through her mind. "Why am I here? What's the point? When will I get to do something that *really* matters?" Chosen for a prestigious internship right out of college, Olivia envisioned being part of work that changed the world. But her days seem to be a string of boring meetings and spreadsheets. She thinks of other friends who went on to seminary or are serving as missionaries. "Lord," she quietly prays, "does my life even have a purpose? I don't understand why you brought me here."

Olivia's thoughts are interrupted as her boss hands out a spreadsheet with columns of figures. As she studies them her heart begins to pound. Something is off, and no one else seems to be raising a red flag. If changes aren't made, thousands of jobs will be at stake. Olivia swallows hard and asks God for extra courage.

Thousands of years before, Esther faced a similar moment. As an attractive, unknown young woman, she was chosen to become the new queen. At first it surely seemed like a glamorous job. But after a year of beauty treatments, a whirlwind wedding, and an inauguration, her life likely settled into a mundane routine. Women didn't have a prominent place in politics, and she probably had to share the affection of her husband with other women. She couldn't even see her royal spouse unless he summoned her. When her cousin Mordecai asked Esther to approach the king because the lives of the Jewish people were being threatened, she revealed, "Thirty days have passed since I was called to go to the king" (Esth. 4:11).

Esther also had to live apart from her people, and no one in the pagan palace even knew her spiritual heritage or cultural origins. Like Olivia, she must have wondered at times, "Lord, why am I here?" God's answer came when Esther learned of a plot by Haman, a government official, to have all the Jews killed. No other Jew had access to the king like she did, and she risked her life to rescue her people. When she expressed uncertainty at first, Mordecai posed a challenging question to her: "Who knows but that you have come to your royal position for such a time as this?" (Esth. 4:14). She then bravely responded, "I will go to the king, even though it is against the law. And if I perish, I perish" (Esth. 4:16).

Situations that call for faith and obedience are still part of our world today. Like Esther did centuries before, Olivia unexpectedly finds herself in a place with access to information that could impact the lives of many. When there's a break in the meeting, she pulls out her phone and texts a friend to say, "Please pray for me. I need to stand up for what's right, and I'm scared. I don't know what's going to happen, but I have to say something." As the team sits down again, she clears her throat, raises her hand, and changes the course of a company and her career.

When we hear stories like Esther's and Olivia's, we can tend to focus on what seems like the "big, world-changing moment" in their lives. But all of the quiet, ordinary days leading up to that were essential too. And they mattered just as much to God. What was true for Olivia and Esther is true for us as well. *God has us where we are today for a purpose to fulfill a part of his plan that only we can.* Our lives are not being wasted. Even the times that don't seem to have as much significance are important preparation for what's coming. We don't need to be doing "greater" things for God. All he asks is for us to love and obey him. As Brother Lawrence said in *The Practice of the Presence of God*, "We ought not to be weary of doing little things for the love of God, who regards not the greatness of the work, but the love with which it is performed."[1]

Here's the secret that Olivia and Esther discovered: *living with purpose simply means living with God.* It means being ready to say yes to whatever he asks us to do, whether it's big or small, quiet or loud, noticeable or invisible. We don't have to find our divine destiny someday, somewhere. We are called "for such a time as this" to such a place as *right here.*

Talk with God about the lies you battle, and ask him to reveal what's true. Listen for his loving voice in your heart, look to his Word, and be honest about what you're feeling.

◆ **What's a Lie I've Battled?** (Example: *My life doesn't have a purpose.*)

◆ **When or How Did I Begin Battling This Lie?** Ask God to bring a specific memory to mind. If one doesn't come, that's totally okay. Just leave this blank.

◆ **How Do I Need to Be Healed from the Ways This Lie Has Wounded Me?** Write a prayer sharing honestly with God about how this lie has hurt you and asking him to heal your heart.

◆ **What's the Truth That Will Defeat This Lie in My Life?** (Example: *I'm here for such a time as this.*) Ask God what's really true, and take time to listen for his answer. It may come from today's Scriptures, the devotional, encouraging words from someone in your life, or his still small voice within your heart.

6

Your Looks Don't Determine Your Worth

"The way I look determines my worth."—Sofia

"Beauty is fleeting; but a woman who fears the LORD is to be praised."
—Proverbs 31 Woman

Read Proverbs 31:10–31

Sofia looks at her reflection in the dressing room and frowns. How could she have gone up a size since last summer? She hears the excited chatter of teenagers as they try on swimsuits and make plans to head to the beach later. She wistfully thinks back to those days when she could eat whatever she wanted and step out on the sand with confidence. Those times are long gone, and while she doesn't mind wearing a cover-up when she visits the water, it bothers her that the desire to cover up in other ways has become more frequent as well. She buys expensive cream to minimize the lines around her eyes. A bad hair day can keep her home from a party. And a dear friend gets avoided at the grocery store when Sofia is wearing sweatpants. She quietly wonders, *Why am I so afraid of not being beautiful?*

It's a question every woman will likely wrestle with at some point in her life. We need to know that even when our looks are gone, we will still be looked on with love. The description of the ideal woman in Proverbs 31 gives us an answer: "Charm is deceptive and beauty is fleeting; but a woman who fears the LORD is to be praised" (Prov. 31:30).

Before we go any further, I have a confession: I've always been intimidated by the Proverbs 31 woman. So before writing this devotional, I decided to do a little research on her. I discovered this: "In traditional Jewish homes, husbands and children recited the poem in Proverbs 31 at the Sabbath table. Written as an acrostic, each line begins with a Hebrew letter in alphabetical sequence, making it easy to memorize."[1] In other words, Proverbs 31 isn't an enormous checklist for one individual. Instead it's a celebration of many different feminine qualities.

Also, this is the only physical description included in the chapter: "She sets about her work vigorously; her arms are strong for her tasks" (v. 17). I'm picturing someone like Rosie the Riveter here! She needs those strong arms because this woman has a life full of action. In this one chapter we find the verbs *brings*, *selects*, *works*, *gets up*, *provides*, *considers*, *plants*, *sees*, *holds*, *grasps*, *extends*, *makes*, *sells*, *supplies*, *speaks*, *watches*, and *fears the Lord*. What's most visible in her life is not her looks but the ways she lives out her faith. She's an example of what Jesus described when he said, "Let your light shine before others, that they may see your good deeds and glorify your Father in heaven" (Matt. 5:16).

How can we beat the fear of our looks fading? *By living in a way that makes others look more at Jesus than at us.* Some of the most beautiful women I've ever met wouldn't be on the cover of a fashion magazine. Yet the wrinkles on their faces are lines in a story of a long, faithful life with Jesus that's truly worth our attention.

Sofia steps out of the dressing room and passes the teenagers on her way to find a better fit. She smiles for a moment and thinks, *Yes, in some ways it would be nice to look like that again. But I wouldn't trade who I've become for the ability to fit into an itsy-bitsy, teeny-weeny bikini.* She seems to silently sense God's affirmation of those thoughts. Surely she grows lovelier to him with every year that goes by as she's conformed even more to the image of his Son. And one day she'll walk along the shore of a heavenly crystal sea looking more beautiful than ever with a heart that's fully clothed in eternal grace and everlasting love.

Truth Your Heart Needs

Talk with God about the lies you battle, and ask him to reveal what's true. Listen for his loving voice in your heart, look to his Word, and be honest about what you're feeling.

◆ **What's a Lie I've Battled?** (Example: *The way I look determines my worth.*)

◆ **When or How Did I Begin Battling This Lie?** Ask God to bring a specific memory to mind. If one doesn't come, that's totally okay. Just leave this blank.

Do You Know You're Already Amazing?

◆ **How Do I Need to Be Healed from the Ways This Lie Has Wounded Me?** Write a prayer sharing honestly with God about how this lie has hurt you and asking him to heal your heart.

◆ **What's the Truth That Will Defeat This Lie in My Life?** (Example: *Beauty is fleeting, but a woman who fears the Lord is to be praised.*) Ask God what's really true, and take time to listen for his answer. It may come from today's Scriptures, the devotional, encouraging words from someone in your life, or his still small voice within your heart.

7

Your God Is Good All the Time

"God is not always good to me."—Naomi

"Even when life is hard, God is still good."—Ruth

Read Ruth 1–4

Naomi opens the cupboard and a few lonely crumbs fall to the floor. Her husband says over her shoulder, "We can't stay here anymore. We have to go to Moab." Naomi silently nods her assent. A famine has come to Israel, and out of desperation her family is choosing to live in a pagan land. Even this beginning to the story in Ruth 1 seems to reveal something about Naomi's outlook. The Jewish people are to live separately from the unbelievers around them. And yet rather than trust that God will ultimately be good to her even in a time of want, Naomi leaves the Promised Land.

Over the next decade Naomi's family seems to be reduced to crumbs as well. She loses her husband and then her sons. She's left with only two gentile daughters-in-law. In those days, women had few ways of providing for themselves and their families. Once again Naomi finds herself in the midst of a famine—only this time it's a personal one. When she hears there is once again food in Israel, she makes plans to return. She urges her daughters-in-law to remain behind, and one complies. But Ruth speaks words of loyalty we still repeat today:

> Don't urge me to leave you or to turn back from you. Where you go I will go, and where you stay I

will stay. Your people will be my people and your God my God. Where you die I will die, and there I will be buried. May the LORD deal with me, be it ever so severely, if even death separates you and me. (Ruth 1:16–17)

Ruth's decision to accompany Naomi is a bold move. It also seems to reveal that even in her wandering and sorrow, Naomi has managed to share the true God with her daughter-in-law. Ruth is choosing to leave all she knows to go to a land where she's not likely to be accepted and has no idea how she'll survive. She makes the opposite choice her mother-in-law did in the beginning: she steps forward in faith, while Naomi fled in fear.

God seems to take note of Ruth's courage and character. A local man named Boaz does as well. Naomi tells Ruth to go find a field to glean grain in so they can have food, knowing that Scripture instructed farmers to leave behind part of their crop for the poor. Through divine providence, Ruth ends up in the field of a distant relative. Not only is Boaz part of her family, he is also

Do You Know You're Already Amazing?

in a position to be Ruth's redeemer. In other words, he had the responsibility to ensure Ruth and Naomi were cared for and the family line was continued. When Ruth reveals this role to Boaz with the guidance of Naomi, he responds with far more than a sense of obligation. He knows Ruth's reputation and has apparently come to have affection for her as she's worked in his fields. Ruth goes from being an outcast to being the beloved wife of a wealthy man, a mother, and the great-grandmother of King David.

When the women in Naomi's town hear the happy news that she has become a grandmother, they say, "Blessed be the LORD, who has not left you this day without a close relative; and may his name be famous in Israel! And may he be to you a restorer of life and a nourisher of your old age; for your daughter-in-law, who loves you, who is better to you than seven sons, has borne him" (Ruth 4:14–15 NKJV). Rather than clinging to crumbs, Naomi finds her life, family, and arms full again. She experiences what her descendant King David will later express in words we can all cling to during the hardest, emptiest moments of our lives: "Give thanks to the LORD, for he is good; his love endures forever. . . . He satisfies the thirsty and fills the hungry with good things" (Ps. 107:1, 9).

Do You Know You're Already Amazing?

Truth Your Heart Needs

Talk with God about the lies you battle, and ask him to reveal what's true. Listen for his loving voice in your heart, look to his Word, and be honest about what you're feeling.

◆ **What's a Lie I've Battled?** (Example: *God is not always good to me.*)

◆ **When or How Did I Begin Battling This Lie?** Ask God to bring a specific memory to mind. If one doesn't come, that's totally okay. Just leave this blank.

◆ **How Do I Need to Be Healed from the Ways This Lie Has Wounded Me?** Write a prayer sharing honestly with God about how this lie has hurt you and asking him to heal your heart.

◆ **What's the Truth That Will Defeat This Lie in My Life?** (Example: *Even when life is hard, God is good.*) Ask God what's really true, and take time to listen for his answer. It may come from today's Scriptures, the devotional, encouraging words from someone in your life, or his still small voice within your heart.

8

You Can Find Satisfaction

"I will never be satisfied."—Samaritan woman at the well

"Only Jesus can truly satisfy me." —Samaritan woman after meeting Jesus

Read John 4:6–42

The noonday sun beats down on her as she makes her daily trip to the well. As she passes open doors, she imagines the whispered conversations inside. Children being warned. Wives spreading gossip. Men making inappropriate remarks. She straightens her shoulders and fixes her eyes on the horizon. Who cares what they say?

She finally arrives at the well and wipes the sweat from her forehead. All the other women in the village come when it's cool, but the heat of the sun is more bearable than the burn of rejection. A memory of watching her mother talk and laugh with friends at the well flashes across her mind. As a little girl she actually believed she'd grow up to be happy and satisfied with her life. What a fool!

Her thoughts are interrupted by a man's voice. Startled, she turns toward the sound and hears the question, "Will you give me a drink?" She knows by his accent that he's Jewish. His people and hers don't mix. Does he think she's a fool too? "You are a Jew and I am a Samaritan woman. How can you ask me for a drink?" she responds (John 4:9).

As if reading her thoughts, he continues, "If you knew the gift of God and who it is that asks you for a drink, you would have asked him and he would have given you living water" (John 4:10).

Do You Know You're Already Amazing?

Yep, he's the religious type. She'll try to ruffle his feathers with questions and maybe he'll go away. Instead he answers, and unlike the other men in her life, he stays.

Then he says something that grabs her attention: "Everyone who drinks this water will be thirsty again, but whoever drinks the water I give them will never thirst. Indeed, the water I give them will become in them a spring of water welling up to eternal life" (John 4:13).

Her heart begins to pound. This is what she wants. To never come to this stupid well again. To have something no one else in this town does so they'll stop looking down on her. To stop being thirsty—*so very thirsty*. She's vowed never to ask a man for anything again, but before she can stop herself, she blurts out, "Sir, give me this water."

The moment the words are out, she hears others hissed to her heart: *This is a righteous man. If he knew your past, he would never give you anything.* She ducks her head in shame and stares at the ground. Sure enough, the man says, "Go get your husband." For a moment she thinks of lying, but a sudden courage seizes her and she tells him—this stranger—the truth. "I have no husband." She wants to add, *I have no one.*

He replies, "You are right when you say you have no husband. The fact is, you have had five husbands, and the man you now have is not your husband. What you have just said is quite true" (John 4:18). It's as if he can see every step of her endless search for something (or someone) to satisfy her soul. She feels a sudden vulnerability and throws another question at him in self-defense. But he remains gentle and kind. Eventually she reveals the hope tucked away in her drained-dry heart: "I know that Messiah is coming" (John 4:25). Maybe there are no good men in this world, but for some inexplicable reason she still believes someday, somehow, one *will* come.

She doesn't expect his reply: "I, the one speaking to you—I am he" (John 4:26).

It's the first time Jesus has ever revealed his true identity to anyone. And the woman who went to the well as an outcast suddenly becomes a chosen messenger. She hurries back to town

Do You Know You're Already Amazing?

and extends a surprising invitation: "Come, see a man who told me everything I ever did. Could this be the Messiah?" (John 4:29).

Maybe the people come because they believe her. Maybe they come because they think they can finally find out all the juicy details of her life. Whatever the reason, many hearts are filled by the time Jesus leaves two days later. "They said to the woman, 'We no longer believe just because of what you said; now we have heard for ourselves, and we know that this man really is the Savior of the world'" (John 4:42).

I like to imagine the Samaritan woman listening to Jesus with the crowd of people from her town. The sun is still high in the sky, but she now has a smile on her face. Perhaps a man taps her on the shoulder and offers her a cup of water with a wink. She's seen that look many times before. But this time she has a different response. She can finally say along with all those who have found soul satisfaction in Jesus, "No thanks— I'm not thirsty."

Truth Your Heart Needs

Talk with God about the lies you battle, and ask him to reveal what's true. Listen for his loving voice in your heart, look to his Word, and be honest about what you're feeling.

◆ **What's a Lie I've Battled?** (Example: *I will never be satisfied.*)

◆ **When or How Did I Begin Battling This Lie?** Ask God to bring a specific memory to mind. If one doesn't come, that's totally okay. Just leave this blank.

Do You Know You're Already Amazing?

◆ **How Do I Need to Be Healed from the Ways This Lie Has Wounded Me?** Write a prayer sharing honestly with God about how this lie has hurt you and asking him to heal your heart.

◆ **What's the Truth That Will Defeat This Lie in My Life?** (Example: *Only Jesus can truly satisfy me.*) Ask God what's really true and take time to listen for his answer. It may come from today's Scriptures, the devotional, encouraging words from someone in your life, or his still small voice within your heart.

9

You're Enough as You Are

"I am enough because of God."—Eve,
before the fall

"I am not enough."—Eve, when the serpent
tempted her

Read Genesis 3

A cool breeze brushes Eve's cheek as she walks
through the Garden of Eden with her husband
and her God. All around her, trees and flowers
bloom in brilliant colors. Animals peacefully

rest in the shade. She breathes in a deep sigh of contentment. *Life is good.* She feels no self-consciousness, worry, or fear. Everything is as it should be. She is loved. She is content. She is safe.

The next day she hears an unfamiliar voice as she picks fruit from a group of trees. "Did God really say, 'You must not eat from any tree in the garden'?" (Gen. 3:1). She furrows her brow and turns to reply. No one has ever questioned God before! She says to the serpent, "We may eat fruit from the trees in the garden, but God did say, 'You must not eat fruit from the tree that is in the middle of the garden, and you must not touch it, or you will die'" (Gen. 3:2–3).

Perhaps she expects this explanation to satisfy this snake in the grass. But he continues, "You will not certainly die. . . . For God knows that when you eat from it your eyes will be opened, and you will be like God, knowing good and evil" (Gen. 3:4–5).

We know how the rest of the story goes. Eve eats and paradise is lost. But what lie entrapped her heart? What did she believe?

When I read this story, one phrase jumps out at me: "you will be like God" (v. 5). In other words, *you're not enough as you are*. And with that lie comes a sinister implication: *God is holding out on you*. Ironically, it's the same reason the serpent fell. Not content with his identity or position in heaven, he grasped for all of God's glory and lost everything. But even then he didn't learn his lesson. He's still trying to drag God's daughters down with him.

When I talk with women as an author, counselor, life coach, and friend, I hear the lie Eve believed repeated so often. And I've heard it in my own heart as well. The enemy has not changed his tactics much since the beginning of time. That one lie has a variety of versions . . .

You're not *lovable* enough.

You're not *good* enough.

You're not *beautiful* enough.

You're not *smart* enough.

You're not *cool* enough.

You're not *successful* enough.

But all of those expressions have the same message. Somehow, in some way, *we must be*

Do You Know You're Already Amazing?

lacking. Who God has made us and what he has given us are not really adequate. That can seem true because we were once all sinners in need of a Savior. But once we give Jesus our lives, he restores all that was lost in the fall. We live in a post-paradise world, but our identities in God's eyes are post-cross perfect. *We are enough because Jesus is enough in us.*

When the enemy tries to convince our hearts that's not true, what can we say in response? He started his temptation of Eve with, "Did God really say . . . ?" I believe we defeat him by answering with "Here's what God really does say. . . ." That's the tactic Jesus used when the devil tempted him.

> Then Jesus was led by the Spirit into the wilderness to be tempted by the devil. After fasting forty days and forty nights, he was hungry. The tempter came to him and said, "If you are the Son of God, tell these stones to become bread."
>
> Jesus answered, "It is written: 'Man shall not live on bread alone, but on every word that comes from the mouth of God.'" (Matt. 4:1–4)

The devil tempted Jesus two more times after that, and our Savior always responded with Scripture. We can follow his example when the enemy tries to ensnare us as well. For example, when we hear the lie, "You are not enough," we can answer with what God says to us through Scriptures like these:

I am fearfully and wonderfully made. (Ps. 139:14)

His divine power has given us everything we need for a godly life. (2 Pet. 1:3)

I can do all this through him who gives me strength. (Phil. 4:13)

The only weapon that's part of the armor of God is "the sword of the Spirit, which is the word of God" (Eph. 6:17). The enemy took advantage of Eve, and she acted as if she were defenseless. But we don't have to do the same. You are a woman. You are a warrior. You wield God's truth, and it cannot be overcome.

Do You Know You're Already Amazing?

Truth Your Heart Needs

Talk with God about the lies you battle and ask him to reveal what's true. Listen for his loving voice in your heart, look to his Word, and be honest about what you're feeling.

◆ **What's a Lie I've Battled?** (Example: *I'm not enough.*)

◆ **When or How Did I Begin Battling This Lie?** Ask God to bring a specific memory to mind. If one doesn't come, that's totally okay. Just leave this blank.

◆ **How Do I Need to Be Healed from the Ways This Lie Has Wounded Me?** Write a prayer sharing honestly with God about how this lie has hurt you and asking him to heal your heart.

◆ **What's the Truth That Will Defeat This Lie in My Life?** (Example: *I am enough because of God.*) Ask God what's really true, and take time to listen for his answer. It may come from today's Scriptures, the devotional, encouraging words from someone in your life, or his still small voice within your heart.

10

You're Never Too Young or Too Old for God to Use You

"God can't use me at my age."—Sarah, when angels announce she'll become a mother in her nineties

"Age isn't a limitation to God."—Sarah, when she gives birth to a son

Read Genesis 18:1–15; 21:1–7

Sarah stands at the opening of the tent and strains to hear the conversation between the men as they talk over a meal. Her hands are still dusty with flour from the bread she's just baked. She glances down at them, and a familiar sadness sweeps over her. These hands have never soothed a baby of her own as he drifts off to sleep. They've never steadied a toddler as he took his first step. They've never patted a young man on his back for a job well done.

She thinks back to the day Abraham rushed home to tell her, "God has promised I will be the father of many nations!" But the years have slipped by, and since Sarah is now a woman in her nineties, it seems the hope of her ever being part of this divine plan Abraham shared is long gone.

One of the men makes a statement, and she tilts her head in confusion. Her hearing must be going as well! But, no, he really did say what she thought: "I will surely return to you about this time next year, and Sarah your wife will have a son" (Gen. 18:10). Before she can help it, a burst of laughter escapes from her lips. A son! A year from now! These men must not understand much about how children come into this world.

She realizes the men have all swiveled their heads to stare at her. "The LORD said to Abraham, 'Why did Sarah laugh and say, "Will I really have a child, now that I am old?" Is anything too hard for the LORD? I will return to you at the appointed time next year, and Sarah will have a son'" (Gen. 18:13). Sarah clears her throat and tries to cover her tracks. "I did not laugh" (Gen. 18:15). But she's not getting away with anything. The God of truth is calling her bluff. "Yes, you did laugh" (Gen. 18:15).

Why does the Lord call Sarah out? It's not to humiliate her. Instead it seems to be a moment of healing and resolution. Ever since Sarah first heard God's promise to Abraham years before, she has wrestled with waiting for it to come true. She even told Abraham to sleep with her maid Hagar to produce an heir (a common practice in that day—although not condoned by God). She may be in her nineties, but the time has finally come to get serious about believing God can and will use her.

We don't know how this conversation ended or how Sarah felt after it occurred. After this brief interaction, she steps off the pages of Scripture for a few chapters, but when we see her again, there is laughter once more.

> Now the LORD was gracious to Sarah as he had said, and the LORD did for Sarah what he had promised. Sarah became pregnant and bore a son to Abraham in his old age, at the very time God had promised him. Abraham gave the name Isaac [which means laughter] to the son Sarah bore him. . . .
>
> Sarah said, "God has brought me laughter, and everyone who hears about this will laugh with me." And she added, "Who would have said to Abraham that Sarah would nurse children? Yet I have borne him a son in his old age." (Gen. 21:1–3, 6–7)

One phrase Sarah uses strikes me: "Who would have said . . . ?" Clearly there's just one possible answer. *Only God.* Only he would have said that a woman in her nineties would become a mother to the covenant son. Only he would have patiently persevered in seeing his plan unfold even when those involved tried to hurry

Do You Know You're Already Amazing?

it and make it happen on their own. Only he would have chosen two imperfect people past their prime to be the spiritual parents of many nations. What we see as limitations, God sees as opportunities to show his glory. We're never too young or old for him to use us. And when it comes to surprising us with the ways he fulfills his promises, he always gets the last laugh.

Truth Your Heart Needs

Talk with God about the lies you battle, and ask him to reveal what's true. Listen for his loving voice in your heart, look to his Word, and be honest about what you're feeling.

◆ **What's a Lie I've Battled?** (Example: *God can't use me at my age.*)

◆ **When or How Did I Begin Battling This Lie?** Ask God to bring a specific memory to mind. If one doesn't come, that's totally okay. Just leave this blank.

Do You Know You're Already Amazing?

◆ **How Do I Need to Be Healed from the Ways This Lie Has Wounded Me?** Write a prayer sharing honestly with God about how this lie has hurt you and asking him to heal your heart.

◆ **What's the Truth That Will Defeat This Lie in My Life?** (Example: *Age isn't a limitation to God.*) Ask God what's really true, and take time to listen for his answer. It may come from today's Scriptures, the devotional, encouraging words from someone in your life, or his still small voice within your heart.

11

You Can Always Make a New Start

"I'm trapped in my sin."—the women of Jericho

"I can make a new start."—Rahab

Read Joshua 2; 6:22–25

Rahab leans back against the pillow and twists a lock of her long, dark hair—a habit when she's thinking. How many times did her mother say to her as a little girl, "Rahab! Stop pulling at your hair!"? She obviously didn't listen to her mother's instructions on that subject . . . or many others. Otherwise she wouldn't be a prostitute with yet another man in her bed talking about the army approaching Jericho. The location of her home and business is close to the city gates where the leaders often meet. And physical intimacy seems to make information flow freely. She knows more than anyone realizes.

The man continues, "Their God dried up the Red Sea, and they walked across on dry land! How are we supposed to fight an enemy with that kind of power?" He shakes his head, rises to put on his clothes, and kisses her on the forehead. "We'd better enjoy ourselves while we can if the end is near! I'll see you next week." She nods her head and gives a weak smile, but her thoughts are far away. She thinks of the other stories she's heard about this God. He is mighty. Holy. It seems he will do anything for his people.

She slips on a robe and goes to the window. Her house is part of the city wall, and she stares toward the horizon where wisps of smoke rise in the distance. A familiar longing seizes her heart.

I want to get out of here. Out of this place. Out of this life. Away from lovers who will never love her. Like a hot coal, a new secret burns inside her. She has become a believer in this foreign God she's heard of but never seen. "Please rescue me," she whispers.

The sound of urgent knocking interrupts her thoughts. She sighs. Another customer. But when she opens the door, she knows instantly these two men are not from her town. The pleading in their eyes confirms there's not much time to act. She rushes the Israelite spies to the roof and hides them not long before messengers from the king arrive. Fortunately, distracting men is one of her specialties, and she talks them into going on a wild goose chase outside the city gates.

As night falls, she goes to the roof to tell the Israelite spies all that's being said and describes the great fear sweeping through the city. Then she finally dares to say out loud what her heart knows is true: "The LORD your God is God in heaven above and on the earth below" (Josh. 2:11). She waits for rebuke or disdain, but when none comes, she adds a plea for deliverance:

Do You Know You're Already Amazing?

"Swear to me by the LORD that you will show kindness to my family, because I have shown kindness to you" (Josh. 2:12). Rahab and the spies make a plan for her to hang a scarlet rope from the window to identify her home (a symbol many scholars believe foreshadows the blood of Christ). All the rumors in Jericho prove true when the city is destroyed, but Rahab and her entire family are spared.

Rahab's story in the book of Joshua ends with, "and she lives among the Israelites to this day" (Josh. 6:25). But we find out more about Rahab's new life in an unexpected place, the genealogy of Christ in the book of Matthew: "Salmon the father of Boaz, *whose mother was Rahab,* Boaz the father of Obed, whose mother was Ruth, Obed the father of Jesse, and Jesse the father of King David" (1:5–6). Although a former prostitute and a gentile, Rahab found grace and acceptance with the people of Israel. She married an Israelite man named Salmon, who was the father of someone we've talked about before: Boaz, the redeemer and husband of Ruth. Perhaps Boaz's compassion and affection for Ruth came in part from having a foreign mother who also left a pagan people for the one true God.

Because she dared to believe life could be different, Rahab the prostitute became the mother-in-law of Ruth, the great-great-grandmother of King David, and one of the only women named in the lineage of Jesus. The scarlet cord she stretched out her window reached through generation after generation and still gives us hope today. No matter where we come from or what we have done, God is always willing to give us a new beginning and a place in his extraordinary, eternal plan.

Truth Your Heart Needs

Talk with God about the lies you battle, and ask him to reveal what's true. Listen for his loving voice in your heart, look to his Word, and be honest about what you're feeling.

◆ **What's a Lie I've Battled?** (Example: *I'm trapped in my sin.*)

◆ **When or How Did I Begin Battling This Lie?** Ask God to bring a specific memory to mind. If one doesn't come, that's totally okay. Just leave this blank.

◆ **How Do I Need to Be Healed from the Ways This Lie Has Wounded Me?** Write a prayer sharing honestly with God about how this lie has hurt you and asking him to heal your heart.

◆ **What's the Truth That Will Defeat This Lie in My Life?** (Example: *I can make a new start.*) Ask God what's really true, and take time to listen for his answer. It may come from today's Scriptures, the devotional, encouraging words from someone in your life, or his still small voice within your heart.

Do You Know You're Already Amazing?

12

Your Home Doesn't Have to Be Perfect

"My home has to be perfect."—Ginny

"My home just needs the presence of Jesus."—Lydia

Read Acts 16:13–15, 40

As Ginny wipes her best serving platter, she catches a hazy glimpse of herself in the surface. She tucks a stray hair behind her ear and is surprised by the look of weariness in her eyes. A high-pitched voice calls out "Mom!" and small hands wrap around her legs. She looks down to see ten sticky fingers clinging to her white capri pants. She'll have to change her clothes, and a group of women from her daughter's school will be here in an hour. "Lord," she sighs, "maybe more than just my pants needs to change. I'm so tired of trying to make my home seem like it's perfect all the time."

Like Ginny, Lydia has had a week full of expectations and obligations. As a prominent businesswoman selling purple cloth in Philippi, she has many demands on her time and energy. Scripture implies she has a family to take care of as well. Perhaps seeking a moment of peace, she finds a grassy spot near the river and listens to the ripples of the water. This wide-open space also attracts religious teachers who preach from the riverbank. She shifts her attention when she hears a man talking about how God sent his Son to die for the sins of the whole world so we could belong to him. A fellow listener tells Lydia the speaker is Paul, a Jewish rabbi who once killed Christians but is now leading people to Christ.

Do You Know You're Already Amazing?

Lydia is intrigued. Although she's "a worshiper of God" she doesn't yet know the whole story about this Messiah named Jesus (Acts 16:14).

As Paul speaks, Lydia's heart readily soaks in every word. Soon she and her entire household become believers and are baptized. She's filled with joy and gratitude. How can she repay Paul and the others traveling with him for what she's received? When she hears Paul doesn't have a place to stay, she has her answer. The author of Acts says, "She invited us to her home. 'If you consider me a believer in the Lord,' she said, 'come and stay at my house.' And she persuaded us" (16:15).

Lydia could have said something like . . .

"I have a guest room that looks like a page from a magazine. Come and stay at my house."

"I can whip up meals better than a chef at a fancy restaurant. Come and stay at my house."

"I have children who are going straight from kindergarten to college because they're so smart and well-behaved. Come and stay at my house."

Instead she simply says, "If you consider me a believer in the Lord, come and stay at my house."

In other words, *what matters most about where I live is not that it's perfect but that the presence of Jesus is in it.* That's good news for us. It means we don't have to decorate beautifully, cook fantastically, and entertain effortlessly before we invite others into our space. (It also means we don't even need an actual house. A dorm room, apartment, high-rise building, hut, or wherever else God has us will work just fine too.)

As Ginny's anxiety reaches its peak, she hears the doorbell ring. It's been a hectic hour, and she hasn't finished everything she hoped. A dirty dish still sits in one side of the sink. A plate of slightly burned cookies accuses her of mistreatment from the counter. A shriek followed by laughter and what sounds like jumping on the bed comes from upstairs. This is not how she pictured the evening beginning. She considers hiding in the pantry and pretending not to be home. Instead she gathers her courage and opens the front door.

A few hours later, as Ginny ushers out her guests, a new friend pauses to talk to her. "Thanks for letting us come over. I'm going through a hard time, and I've been feeling like a failure because my life isn't perfect. It means a lot to see you're real and you can relate. Being here helped me feel better."

As Ginny walks back toward her still-messy kitchen, she has a different perspective. It no longer matters that her refreshments didn't turn out just right or that stray toys are still scattered across the living room. What matters is that she provided a space for Jesus to love on people— even if her friend doesn't fully realize that's what happened yet. The burden of expectations carried far too long slips from Ginny's shoulders as she realizes what Lydia knew: *true hospitality just means opening our homes the same way we open our hearts.* Jesus dwells in both, and he'll take care of what matters most.

Truth Your Heart Needs

Talk with God about the lies you battle, and ask him to reveal what's true. Listen for his loving voice in your heart, look to his Word, and be honest about what you're feeling.

◆ **What's a Lie I've Battled?** (Example: *My home has to be perfect.*)

◆ **When or How Did I Begin Battling This Lie?** Ask God to bring a specific memory to mind. If one doesn't come, that's totally okay. Just leave this blank.

Do You Know You're Already Amazing?

◆ **How Do I Need to Be Healed from the Ways This Lie Has Wounded Me?** Write a prayer sharing honestly with God about how this lie has hurt you and asking him to heal your heart.

◆ **What's the Truth That Will Defeat This Lie in My Life?** (Example: *My home just needs the presence of Jesus.*) Ask God what's really true, and take time to listen for his answer. It may come from today's Scriptures, the devotional, encouraging words from someone in your life, or his still small voice within your heart.

Your Home Doesn't Have to Be Perfect

13

You Belong

"I don't belong."—Carrie

"God has a place for me."—Anna

Read Luke 2:36–38

Carrie grips the edges of her lunch tray and takes a deep breath. *Worst part of the day,* she thinks. As she walks past each table, she tries to offer a smile and make eye contact. But heads stay lowered and conversations continue. She should be used to this by now since her dad's job requires them to move often and she's perpetually "the new kid." It doesn't help that she doesn't wear the right jeans, have a cool phone, or listen to the latest music. But she still dreams of faces who are glad to see her, hands waving her over to a spot that's been saved for her, and the feeling that she fits.

Once youthful like Carrie, at age eighty-four Anna no longer has the coordination or balance she used to possess. She steadies herself on a wall of the temple court before she takes the next step toward her favorite spot to pray. As she rests, she thinks briefly of her seven-year marriage. Life would have been very different if her young husband had lived. Or if they'd had children before he died. But now she wouldn't trade anything for what God has given her—an opportunity to spend her every waking moment fully devoted to him.

A fresh-faced couple walks past her holding a baby boy. It's a scene she witnesses daily since the law requires that "every firstborn male is to be consecrated to the Lord" (Luke 2:23). But something seems different this time. A prophetess accustomed to hearing God's voice, Anna quiets her heart so she can listen. Then a wide smile spreads across her face. She suddenly feels like a young girl again and practically races toward the family. "She gave thanks to God and spoke about the child to all who were looking forward to the redemption of Jerusalem" (Luke 2:38).

Anna can see from the parents' faces that much of this is still a mystery to them. In many ways, it is to her as well. But what's absolutely clear is this: God has put her in the perfect place at the perfect time to witness a miracle. She thinks of the dark days after her husband's death. Relatives urged her to marry again. "A woman without a husband or children has no place in our society," they told her. "How will you survive? What will give your life meaning? Who will take care of you when you're old?" they asked. The words were spoken out of concern and during that time of history had an unfortunate ring of truth to them.

But in the stillness of the night when her tears had dried, Anna sensed a gentle invitation. "I have a place for you," God seemed to say. So despite all the advice, she went to God's house instead of the home of a new husband. "She never left the temple but worshiped night and day, fasting and praying" (Luke 2:37).

In her most human moments, Anna wondered if everyone had been right. Her life had been far from "normal," after all. She'd never been able to relate with her peers. She didn't fit her culture's expectations or standards for women. But today she knows with everything in her being that she's exactly where God wants her. She thinks of David's words, "Better is one day in your courts than a thousand elsewhere" (Ps. 84:10). She has not been *left out*—she has been *let in* on God's extraordinary secret. The Messiah has come! *It has all been worth it.*

Carrie whispers *"It has all been worth it"* too as she sits in front of a canvas to paint years later. She thinks about the lonely moments. The long walks. The unexpected refuge she found in her sketchpad. Would she be who she is today without them? She doubts it. Now that she's a well-known artist, people seek Carrie out. At a recent school reunion hosted at a high-end venue, a large painting of hers hung behind the area where they had dinner. Her peers vied for her attention and gushed about her talent. She silently laughed at the irony: she finally had a seat at the table. The uncertain young girl in the lunchroom would have leaped into it and clung to it with all her heart. But the grown-up woman she's become doesn't need it. She knows her identity and worth come from God. All the rejection she faced drove her right into his wide-open arms, and she's stayed there ever since.

We can spend a lifetime asking, "Where do I belong?" Or, like Carrie and Anna, we can come to believe all we really need to know is, "*Who* do I belong to?" God wants to answer that question every time our insecure, searching hearts ask it and to give us a place with him forever.

Do You Know You're Already Amazing?

Truth Your Heart Needs

Talk with God about the lies you battle, and ask him to reveal what's true. Listen for his loving voice in your heart, look to his Word, and be honest about what you're feeling.

◆ **What's a Lie I've Battled?** (Example: *I don't belong.*)

◆ **When or How Did I Begin Battling This Lie?** Ask God to bring a specific memory to mind. If one doesn't come, that's totally okay. Just leave this blank.

◆ **How Do I Need to Be Healed from the Ways This Lie Has Wounded Me?** Write a prayer sharing honestly with God about how this lie has hurt you and asking him to heal your heart.

◆ **What's the Truth That Will Defeat This Lie in My Life?** (Example: *God has a place for me.*) Ask God what's really true, and take time to listen for his answer. It may come from today's Scriptures, the devotional, encouraging words from someone in your life, or his still small voice within your heart.

Do You Know You're Already Amazing?

14

You Can Come to Jesus as You Are

"I have to get it together before I come to Jesus."—Brittney

"If I come to Jesus as I am, he will make me whole."—the woman who had been bleeding for twelve years

Read Mark 5:25–34

Brittney glances around the group of women gathered in a living room for a Bible study. Her neighbor has been inviting her for months, and she's finally agreed to come—mostly in the hopes she'll stop being asked. She looks at the wide smiles, cute outfits, and carefully done hair. *These women have it all together,* she thinks. *If they knew who I really am and all I've been through, they'd never let me near them.* A childhood full of abuse. Poor choices with teenage boys, then grown men. Addiction to numb the pain. It seems her whole life she's been hiding something, and shame is her most constant companion. Maybe one day she can be good enough for God to want her.

Shame is a familiar friend to the woman standing at the edge of a crowd on the dusty streets of Israel as well. She thinks back to the first day she noticed the red spot on her robe at a time when she wasn't expecting her monthly period. Concerned, she asked the other women in her family about it. Her mother, grandmother, and sisters reassured her there was nothing to fear. This happened to women sometimes. Jewish law said she was unclean for that day, but surely it would go away. But their comforting words turned out to be in vain as that one day turned into a dozen years.

Twelve years of suffering and pain.

Twelve years of doctors invading every part of her body.

Twelve years of being unclean in the eyes of those around her.

Although Scripture didn't say so, people in that time commonly assumed physical illness was connected to spiritual failure. She knows there must be whispered conversations about what she must have done to bring this on herself—especially since no doctor she'd gone to could cure her. *Maybe they're right about me*, she thinks. She's come to find out once and for all. She shouldn't even be here since she could defile everyone around her. But she's desperate.

She pushes in until only a foot or so remains between her and Jesus. Everyone has been talking about him too. They believe he could be the Messiah. But will he be *her* Savior? Her hand trembles and she considers turning back, but what would she return to? More pain? A life of being alone? The feeling she will never be good enough? She takes a deep breath and reaches out. Her fingers skim the edge of his cloak. It's only a second before he takes the next step and it swishes beyond her reach. But it's enough. She feels an indescribable warmth flow through her, filling her with a wholeness beyond anything she's ever known. She's healed!

Just then Jesus asks a question. "'Who touched my clothes?' 'You see the people crowding against you,' his disciples answered, 'and yet you can ask, 'Who touched me?' But Jesus kept looking around to see who had done it. Then the woman, knowing what had happened to her, came and fell at his feet and, trembling with fear, told him the whole truth. He said to her, 'Daughter, your faith has healed you. Go in peace and be freed from your suffering'" (Mark 5:30–34). Pause for a moment and consider this phrase: she *told him the whole truth.* Yes, she'd already received her physical healing. But I believe Jesus stopped and sought her out because he knew she needed to *tell him everything* for her heart and soul to heal as well.

The words spill from Brittney's lips. She keeps telling herself to stop. She doesn't know these

Do You Know You're Already Amazing?

women. She shouldn't trust them. They'll just be more names to add to her long list of rejections. But when she finally looks up, their perfect mascara is smeared, and they're looking at her like they know what it means to be broken too. Her neighbor asks, "Can I pray for you?" and when Brittney nods, a gentle hand reaches out to rest on her knee, just above the hole where jagged threads spill out. She can't remember the last time anyone touched her without their own selfish reasons.

As her neighbor murmurs words about how Brittney is loved, accepted, and chosen, a strange feeling flows through her. She can sense it seeping into all the cracks in her heart. After "amen," Brittney looks up with wonder in her eyes. "What was that all about?" she asks. The women laugh and she joins them. She doesn't fully understand what just happened, but she knows this: for the first time the shame is inexplicably, gloriously gone.

The woman with the issue of blood "suffered a great deal under the care of many doctors and had spent all she had" (Mark 5:26). Brittney had many "doctors," like sex, substances, and isolation, who cost her dearly and only made her worse as well. We are all drawn to false physicians who promise quick cures but leave us more broken than before. Only Jesus can heal every part of us. Let's dare to reach out and tell the whole truth to the One who can make us truly whole.

Truth Your Heart Needs

Talk with God about the lies you battle, and ask him to reveal what's true. Listen for his loving voice in your heart, look to his Word, and be honest about what you're feeling.

◆ **What's a Lie I've Battled?** (Example: *I have to get it together before I come to Jesus.*)

◆ **When or How Did I Begin Battling This Lie?** Ask God to bring a specific memory to mind. If one doesn't come, that's totally okay. Just leave this blank.

◆ **How Do I Need to Be Healed from the Ways This Lie Has Wounded Me?** Write a prayer sharing honestly with God about how this lie has hurt you and asking him to heal your heart.

◆ **What's the Truth That Will Defeat This Lie in My Life?** (Example: *If I come to Jesus as I am, he will make me whole.*) Ask God what's really true, and take time to listen for his answer. It may come from today's Scriptures, the devotional, encouraging words from someone in your life, or his still small voice within your heart.

15

You Have Something Valuable to Give

"I don't have much to offer."—Shannon

"God can use whatever I have to give."
—the widow who gave two coins

Read Mark 12:41–44

Shannon studies the collection of ornate frames hanging on the wall in her father's office. One holds her oldest brother's diploma. Another displays a picture of her younger sister hoisting a blue ribbon high in the air. A third contains a certificate of excellence Shannon's twin received after recent achievements for her company. Although present in family pictures, Shannon is notably absent here. Her unseen, unglamorous work at a nonprofit organization doesn't give her father big reasons to brag. In his eyes, she has fallen short in comparison with her siblings. She sighs and thinks of what he said to her at dinner last week: "I just hope you're not throwing away your life."

A widow steps into the temple court and takes in the familiar scene before her. She clings to prayer and worship when worry and sorrow try to overwhelm her. So much slipped away with her husband's last breath. Financial security. The sense of purpose and pride in her role as a wife. Her standing in the community. Even in this holy place, she sometimes feels as if she doesn't belong anymore. Pharisees in flowing robes that cost more than her monthly budget stand in one corner arguing a religious point. A well-dressed couple with heads held high and smiles on their faces greet friends. Her neighbor vies for the

Do You Know You're Already Amazing?

attention of an important official. As she watches, everyone slowly makes their way to the treasury where offerings are collected. She almost gasps at the amount of money each noisily puts in when it's their turn.

The two small coins she's carried with her seem to burn into the palm of her hand. Who is she kidding? No one needs what she has to give. Maybe she should just go back home and tuck her tiny treasure away. It won't be missed. She probably won't be either. Surely God will understand. But she knows in her heart this isn't about impressing anyone. It's an act of trust, love, and obedience. She squares her shoulders and marches forward. "Lord, you are my provider," she whispers as she drops the coins. "All I have, all I am is yours."

As she turns back, she sees she's not the only one who has been watching the offerings. A group of men are observing as well, and one with kind eyes gives her an understanding smile. She hears him say to those gathered around him, "Truly I tell you, this poor widow has put more into the treasury than all the others. They all gave out of their wealth; but she, out of her poverty, put in everything—all she had to live on" (Mark 12:43–44). Where has she seen him before? Oh, yes, this is Jesus! The one many believe to be the Messiah. He has noticed her. He has seen the sacrifice. He grasps the true value of what she's giving. Even if no one else understands, his affirmation somehow seems like enough.

Shannon hears her phone beep and glances down to see a photo appear on the screen. It's one of her team members with her arms wrapped around a small, smiling child. She recognizes this little one. Not long ago her ribs showed through a thin, dirty dress and her eyes were round hollows empty of hope. But now her cheeks are full, and she seems to be clapping her hands at some unseen wonder. Shannon holds the phone out a bit to get a better look. As she does, she realizes it almost appears as if the photo is part of the wall of frames. She thinks of the many "golden opportunities" she turned down to take the far-from-fancy path that has led her to this moment. And suddenly she knows: there's not an offer in this world that can compare with offering herself to the God who loves her.

Do You Know You're Already Amazing?

Shannon and the widow with two coins understood there's only one thing we can give to God that he doesn't already have: *our hearts*. That means we all have something valuable to offer. And with him, a little can be so much more than we see.

Truth Your Heart Needs

Talk with God about the lies you battle, and ask him to reveal what's true. Listen for his loving voice in your heart, look to his Word, and be honest about what you're feeling.

◆ **What's a Lie I've Battled?** (Example: *I don't have much to offer.*)

◆ **When or How Did I Begin Battling This Lie?** Ask God to bring a specific memory to mind. If one doesn't come, that's totally okay. Just leave this blank.

Do You Know You're Already Amazing?

◆ **How Do I Need to Be Healed from the Ways This Lie Has Wounded Me?** Write a prayer sharing honestly with God about how this lie has hurt you and asking him to heal your heart.

◆ **What's the Truth That Will Defeat This Lie in My Life?** (Example: *God can use whatever I have to give.*) Ask God what's really true, and take time to listen for his answer. It may come from today's Scriptures, the devotional, encouraging words from someone in your life, or his still small voice within your heart.

16

You Can Trust
God's Timing

*"Jesus is late."—Mary, the sister of
Lazarus, before he was resurrected*

*"I can trust Jesus' timing."—Mary,
the sister of Lazarus, after he was resurrected*

Read John 11:1–44

Mary stares out the window as memories flash
through her mind like scenes from a too-good-
to-be-true story. Sitting at the feet of Jesus,

transfixed by his words, while her sister Martha remained distracted by preparations. Listening to laughter as he and the disciples shared meals with her family. Hearing him knock often on the door of their home and answering with joy. She would give anything to hear the sounds of his arrival now. Where was he? Why hadn't he come? Yes, she believed he was the chosen Messiah. But she also thought he was a true friend who would rush to their sides as soon as they sent word Lazarus was sick.

But he hadn't been there when she and Martha took turns watching over Lazarus through the night. He hadn't been there as their brother drew his last ragged breath. He hadn't been there when the mourners arrived and filled the house with wailing. Or when the rock closed the tomb like a period at the end of a tragic sentence. She had returned home with a broken heart, her red-rimmed eyes still scanning the empty horizon. What if he never came and her faith quietly, unexpectedly slipped away just like her brother?

Suddenly the door swings open. Martha, so often in action and out of breath, pulls her sister aside and confides, "The Teacher is here . . . and is asking for you" (John 11:28). Mary rushes toward the road, carrying a hundred unspoken prayers in her heart. Yet when she's finally in front of Jesus, her sobs choke out all but the one that has haunted her most since they sent for him. "Lord, if you had been here, my brother would not have died" (John 11:32).

Jesus doesn't offer answers. He doesn't try to dry her tears. He doesn't spout off a spiritual cliché. Instead he weeps along with her. The tears of a compassionate friend. The tears of a tender God. The tears of someone who understands the pain of death. Then he asks a simple question: "Where have you laid him?" (John 11:33). He asks us the same. As Joanna Weaver says in *Lazarus Awakening*,

> *Where have you laid your pain?* Jesus asks us tenderly. *Where do you keep all your shattered hopes and dreams? Where have you laid the part of you that died when you were abandoned, forgotten, betrayed? Where are you entombed and enslaved, hemmed in, shut down, and closed off?*
> Come and see, Lord.

Do You Know You're Already Amazing?

That's the only response we need to give.
Come and see.[1]

Jesus does come. And he does see. With eyes that stretch beyond humanity and into eternity. As a quote by Gracie Allen hanging on my mama's refrigerator says, "Never place a period where God has placed a comma."[2] We all have a Lazarus in our lives. A dream that seems to have gasped its final breath. A hope that's lifeless and still. A relationship that seems beyond resurrection. A situation where we echo the words of Mary, "Jesus, if you had really been here for me, then this wouldn't have happened."

But even if his timing is different than ours, Jesus will never abandon us. And when he shows up, you can be sure the show isn't over. After he weeps with his friends by the tomb, he calls Lazarus to come forth. *And suddenly the period placed by humanity becomes an exclamation point inserted by divinity.*

We have the same hope that Mary did, even if it feels delayed sometimes: *Jesus is coming.* He knows our hurt and he cries with us. He has not forgotten us. He will not leave us alone when we're in need. The Author of Life is still asking, "Where have you laid your Lazarus?" He's willing to go with us to the places of our pain. He doesn't fear what he might find. He isn't overwhelmed by the impossibility of our problems. He isn't shocked by our emotions, questions, or even doubts. Whether in this life or the next, he promises to tenderly, powerfully transform our stories in ways beyond what we may even have dared to hope.

Do You Know You're Already Amazing?

Truth Your Heart Needs

Talk with God about the lies you battle, and ask him to reveal what's true. Listen for his loving voice in your heart, look to his Word, and be honest about what you're feeling.

◆ **What's a Lie I've Battled?** (Example: *Jesus is late.*)

◆ **When or How Did I Begin Battling This Lie?** Ask God to bring a specific memory to mind. If one doesn't come, that's totally okay. Just leave this blank.

◆ **How Do I Need to Be Healed from the Ways This Lie Has Wounded Me?** Write a prayer sharing honestly with God about how this lie has hurt you and asking him to heal your heart.

◆ **What's the Truth That Will Defeat This Lie in My Life?** (Example: *I can trust Jesus' timing.*) Ask God what's really true, and take time to listen for his answer. It may come from today's Scriptures, the devotional, encouraging words from someone in your life, or his still small voice within your heart.

Do You Know You're Already Amazing?

17

You're Worth Protecting

"I'm not worth protecting."—the Shulamite woman before meeting her beloved

"I'm loved and cherished."—the Shulamite woman after meeting her beloved

Read Song of Solomon 1–2

"Get up!" the angry voice bellows into her bedroom. The Shulamite woman (let's call her "Shula" for short) startles awake and glimpses the first streaks of sunlight slipping past the curtains. Her stepbrother stands in the doorway with a scowl on his face. "You're going to work in the vineyards again today," he tells her. She tries to protest. "I'm a member of this family—not a servant!" But he cuts her off before she can say more. "You're nothing to us. You can drop dead of a heatstroke for all we care."

Tears flow down Shula's sunburned cheeks, and she catches a glimpse of herself in the mirror. Young women in her culture were supposed to take special care of their skin. Families understood this and took pride in preserving the pretty complexions of their sisters and daughters who would one day become brides. Shula's weather-worn face said so much without a word: I'm unloved. I'm exposed. *I'm not worth protecting.* It seems she often had to offer an explanation for her appearance:

> Don't stare at me because I am dark—
>   the sun has darkened my skin.
> My brothers were angry with me;
>   they forced me to care for their
>   vineyards,

Do You Know You're Already Amazing?

so I couldn't care for myself—my own
vineyard.
Song of Solomon 1:6 NLT

Apparently the original Cinderella is found
not in the pages of a fairy tale but in one of the
most poetic books of Scripture. Like the Cinderella we all know, Shula somehow found an inner
strength that never let the mistreatment she endured fully take away her confidence. She still
declares, "Dark am I, yet lovely" (Song of Sol.
1:5). The man who falls in love with her agrees
and says, "How beautiful you are, my darling!"
(Song of Sol. 1:15). He also says: "Catch for us the
foxes, the little foxes, that ruin the vineyards, our
vineyards that are in bloom" (Song of Sol. 2:15).
That statement may seem insignificant and even
a little strange, but it expresses so much.

In Song of Solomon, the word *vineyards* is
used literally. But it is also used symbolically
when Shula talks about *her* vineyard and when
her beloved describes *their* vineyard. Unlike her
stepbrothers, the beloved sees Shula as well as
their life together as having great value and

being worthy of protection. He truly cherishes her. Yet he doesn't pull a Prince Charming by saying, "Poor thing. You've been through so much! You need someone to rescue you and pamper you the rest of your life." Instead he affirms Shula's strength and competence. He sees her not as a victim but as a beautiful victor. And it appears his affirming love changes the view she has of herself as well.

Many scholars believe Song of Solomon is a metaphor for our relationship with Jesus. We are Shula and Jesus is the beloved. He knows we have been through a lot. He understands we may feel as if our experiences make us unacceptable. He grasps that others have not treated us like the gifts we are. He also sees our true loveliness and celebrates it. And, I believe, like Shula's beloved, Jesus tells us to "catch the foxes that ruin the vineyard." In other words, we're to take action to keep what's destructive (including the harmful behavior of others) from ruining our lives and what we share with him.

It's essential for those of us who have felt helpless when others mistreated us to know Jesus

Do You Know You're Already Amazing?

gives us permission to protect ourselves and what we value. When we are children and hard things happen, we often don't have a choice. And if you have been abused, *it is not your fault*. Thankfully, as adults we do gain power we didn't have before. We can now say, "No, that is not okay. I will not allow you to talk to me or treat me that way."

We don't have to wait on a magical glass slipper before our story changes. Instead we can respectfully and firmly put our foot down where we are today. As Shula's better-than-a-fairy-tale story shows us, we are more resilient than we may have realized. We have greater worth than we may have been led to believe. And we are loved far more than we may have ever thought we deserved. *We are worth protecting.*

Truth Your Heart Needs

Talk with God about the lies you battle, and ask him to reveal what's true. Listen for his loving voice in your heart, look to his Word, and be honest about what you're feeling.

◆ **What's a Lie I've Battled?** (Example: *I'm not worth protecting.*)

◆ **When or How Did I Begin Battling This Lie?** Ask God to bring a specific memory to mind. If one doesn't come, that's totally okay. Just leave this blank.

◆ **How Do I Need to Be Healed from the Ways This Lie Has Wounded Me?** Write a prayer sharing honestly with God about how this lie has hurt you and asking him to heal your heart.

◆ **What's the Truth That Will Defeat This Lie in My Life?** (Example: *I'm loved and cherished.*) Ask God what's really true, and take time to listen for his answer. It may come from today's Scriptures, the devotional, encouraging words from someone in your life, or his still small voice within your heart.

18

Your Needs and Desires Matter

"Having needs and desires is wrong and a burden to others."—Lisa

"Having needs and desires can draw me closer to God and bless others."
—the queen of Sheba

Read 1 Kings 10:1–13

Lisa's grandmother grips her small hand tightly and leans over to whisper in her ear. "Children should be seen and not heard. Do you understand?" Lisa nods as the doors to the reception hall swing open. She's stunned by all she sees. A chocolate fountain. Trays stacked high with cookies. A cake covered with intricate flowers made of icing. Grandma often goes to events with her "society" friends, but this wedding is the first time Lisa has been allowed to tag along. She reaches out to take one of the treats, but a stern look from her grandmother makes her shrink back. At some point she's handed a small plate of food, and even though her tummy still rumbles when they leave, she doesn't ask for more.

As the years go by, Lisa often thinks back on that reception. Was that when she decided discounting her needs and holding back were the safest options? Or was it all the times she tried to get her mother's attention but lost to the open bottle on the table? That ended when she went to live with Grandma. But the immaculate rooms and delicate antiques taught her to soften her steps and lower her voice. Her husband often says to her, "You can tell me what you want" when she responds, "I don't care" to simple questions like which restaurant she'd prefer. And the truth is, she *does* care. But her needs and desires have been buried so long it feels exhausting to excavate them at this stage in her life. She also seems to get a lot of affirmation for her agreeableness, especially at church. "Lisa is so sweet!" the women all say. Yet she has an uneasy awareness of resentment, almost like a new hunger, growing inside.

In spite of her position and possessions, the queen of Sheba also had an increasing sense of dissatisfaction within her. After hearing of King Solomon's wisdom, she thought he might be able to give her what she sought, so she made plans to visit his kingdom. After a long journey, she stepped through his doors and discovered a scene more elaborate than any wedding reception. "When the queen of Sheba saw all the wisdom of Solomon and the palace he had built, the food on his table, the seating of his officials, the attending servants in their robes, his cupbearers, and the burnt offerings he made at the temple of the LORD, *she was overwhelmed*" (1 Kings 10:4–5).

The queen could have turned back at that moment. Perhaps she had the fleeting thought,

Do You Know You're Already Amazing?

What if I'm bothering this busy, important man?
But she pressed forward. She "came to Solomon
and talked with him about all that she had on
her mind" and he "answered all her questions"
(1 Kings 10:2–3). What she wanted most were not
the treasures of earth but those of heaven. And
her boldness was richly rewarded. As Liz Curtis
Higgs says in *It's Good to Be Queen*, "Boldness
doesn't mean having a big ego. Being arrogant,
conceited, or self-centered. Acting in a forward,
boastful or pushy manner. . . . True boldness is
God at work in us."[1] In other words, *righteous
boldness is having the courage to pursue God's
best for our lives.*

The queen of Sheba shows us we're to identify
what we want and when it aligns with God's will
to audaciously go for it. Jesus said, "Ask and it
will be given to you; seek and you will find; knock
and the door will be opened to you" (Matt. 7:7).
When we do so, we are creating an opportunity
for God to use us to bless others. "King Solomon gave the queen of Sheba all she desired
and asked for, besides what he had given her out
of his royal bounty. Then she left and returned

with her retinue to her own country" (1 Kings 10:13). When the queen went home, she didn't go empty-handed. She brought lavish gifts from Solomon, wisdom that would help her rule well, and a new faith in the one true God. All of those benefited her people. *When we deny our needs and desires, we're not the only ones who miss out.*

Unlike Lisa's grandmother, God is inviting us to enjoy our fill of his abundant goodness. And as the queen of Sheba found, we will have plenty to share with others too. Our needs and desires can't diminish or detract from the divine supply. God's provision is limitless. No heart is required to go hungry. There truly is more than enough for all of us.

Truth Your Heart Needs

Talk with God about the lies you battle, and ask him to reveal what's true. Listen for his loving voice in your heart, look to his Word, and be honest about what you're feeling.

◆ **What's a Lie I've Battled?** (Example: *Having needs and desires is wrong and a burden to others.*)

◆ **When or How Did I Begin Battling This Lie?** Ask God to bring a specific memory to mind. If one doesn't come, that's totally okay. Just leave this blank.

◆ **How Do I Need to Be Healed from the Ways This Lie Has Wounded Me?** Write a prayer sharing honestly with God about how this lie has hurt you and asking him to heal your heart.

◆ **What's the Truth That Will Defeat This Lie in My Life?** (Example: *Having needs and desires can draw me closer to God and bless others.*) Ask God what's really true, and take time to listen for his answer. It may come from today's Scriptures, the devotional, encouraging words from someone in your life, or his still small voice within your heart.

Do You Know You're Already Amazing?

19

You Know More than You Think

"I'm not smart enough."—Cindy

"God makes me wise."—the voice of wisdom

Read Proverbs 8

Cindy's eyes fill with tears as the tests are handed back to the class. Another red *F* jumps out from the top of hers like an accusation. It's not just a grade anymore—the word *failure* has become a label stuck to her heart. It will be years before she finds out she has a learning disability. Treatment and tutoring make the *F*s disappear, but the shame still remains.

Eventually Cindy graduates and gets a job she loves. But anytime she's asked to provide an answer or make a decision, the old fear comes rushing back. Her boss often tells her, "Trust what you think is best. You know more than you think you do." Cindy is also part of a women's study at church. She diligently completes each lesson, but every week she sits quietly while others speak up. What if what she's written down is wrong? Then the group around her could turn out to be just like her former classmates who mocked her. One week her study leader pulls her aside and says, "You have so much to offer. I hope one day you feel like you can share your heart with us." Cindy desperately hopes the same.

What Cindy hasn't realized yet is that there's something even better than being seen as "smart." It's being *wise*. Intelligence comes from genetics. Knowledge comes from books. But wisdom can only come from God. My definition of wisdom is

Do You Know You're Already Amazing?

simply this: *understanding how to apply truth.* It's head knowledge lived out through our hearts and hands. Proverbs, the book of wisdom, includes two dialogues by "The Voice of Wisdom." And I love this—*Wisdom is a woman.* She extends this open invitation: "Listen, for I have trustworthy things to say; I open my lips to speak what is right. My mouth speaks what is true" (Prov. 8:6–7). She can be found anywhere by anyone.

My husband and I recently traveled to the Dominican Republic with Compassion International. During our time there we visited families with children sponsored through Compassion's program. I met one grandmother who lived in a box-like hut on the edge of the river and spent all her time caring for her disabled granddaughter. This older woman's eyes shone with joy. Although I doubt she had any formal education, it was clear she knew what mattered most in this life. I noticed a single word written next to the only window in her home. As I leaned in closer I realized what it said: *Jesus.* He was the source of the light in this tiny dwelling. And the source of the wisdom in this woman's soul. At that moment

You Know More than You Think

I realized all over again: true success in life isn't about how much you know—it's about *Who* you know.

In contrast, a magazine I flipped through on the trip home featured a socialite who had everything at her fingertips. Endless financial resources. The best education. The most sought-after opportunities. Yet the answers she longed for most still seemed to elude her. She shared confusion and hurt over another relationship ending, her latest trip to rehab, and a constant fear of the future. I wondered, "Who is truly poor—the grandmother in the shack or the socialite in her penthouse apartment?" As Solomon says, "Blessed are those who find wisdom, those who gain understanding, for she is more profitable than silver and yields better returns than gold. She is more precious than rubies; nothing you desire can compare with her" (Prov. 3:13–15).

For Cindy, a grandmother in the Dominican Republic, the socialite, and all of us, here's the great news: wisdom is available to everyone. It's not limited by our level of education, learning ability, or status in society. The voice of wisdom is still speaking today, and we're all invited to listen. We don't have to fear being shamed, turned away, or told, "You should know that already." Scripture tells us, "If any of you lacks wisdom, you should ask God, who gives generously to all *without finding fault*, and it will be given to you" (James 1:5).

God is not holding a divine red pen and waiting to write *F*s on our attempts at finding answers. Instead he's a patient teacher who's ready and willing to share all we need to know to discover his very best for our lives.

Truth Your Heart Needs

Talk with God about the lies you battle, and ask him to reveal what's true. Listen for his loving voice in your heart, look to his Word, and be honest about what you're feeling.

◆ **What's a Lie I've Battled?** (Example: *I'm not smart enough.*)

◆ **When or How Did I Begin Battling This Lie?** Ask God to bring a specific memory to mind. If one doesn't come, that's totally okay. Just leave this blank.

Do You Know You're Already Amazing?

◆ **How Do I Need to Be Healed from the Ways This Lie Has Wounded Me?** Write a prayer sharing honestly with God about how this lie has hurt you and asking him to heal your heart.

◆ **What's the Truth That Will Defeat This Lie in My Life?** (Example: *God makes me wise.*) Ask God what's really true, and take time to listen for his answer. It may come from today's Scriptures, the devotional, encouraging words from someone in your life, or his still small voice within your heart.

20

You Can Take God at His Word

"I'm not sure God can do what he says."
—Elizabeth's husband, Zechariah

"God will do whatever he says."
—Mary, the mother of Jesus

Read Luke 1:5–38

Elizabeth and Zechariah sit at the breakfast table and talk about the coming day. A bit of early morning light hits the two empty chairs beside them, and Elizabeth's thoughts drift toward the past. She thinks of when she and Zechariah hoped, prayed, and pleaded for God to fill their family with children. Yet the years went by and her womb remained closed. Slowly they had come to accept that God had a different plan than they imagined, but sometimes the ache returned. Zechariah recognizes the far-off look on his wife's face. He gently covers her hand with his and whispers, "God has been good to us." She nods and kisses him on the cheek. He says, "I'm heading to the temple—I've been chosen to burn incense before the Lord today." Elizabeth rises and escorts her husband to the door. As he leaves she replies, "It's always an honor to be chosen by the Lord."

Although we don't know all that happened before Zechariah performed his priestly duties that day, perhaps words like those did ring in his ears. His life was a paradox: picked by God to be a priest, yet passed over when it came to being a father. *Until now.* An angel appears before Zechariah at the temple and tells him, "Do not be afraid, Zechariah; your prayer has been

You Can Take God at His Word

heard. Your wife Elizabeth will bear you a son, and you are to call him John. He will be a joy and delight to you, and many will rejoice because of his birth" (Luke 1:13–14).

Zechariah and Elizabeth were a godly couple, and Scripture even says, "Both of them were righteous in the sight of God, observing all the Lord's commands and decrees blamelessly" (Luke 1:6). Yet the faith of the man who will be the father of John the Baptist, the cousin of Jesus, falters in this important moment. Perhaps after all the years of infertility, this is the one area of his life where he questions what God can do. Whatever the cause, the angel says, "You will be silent and not able to speak until the day this happens, because you did not believe my words, which will come true at their appointed time" (Luke 1:20).

Fast-forward to a similar scene. Same angel. Same announcement of a baby coming. Completely different response. Mary, a young, unmarried woman, is told, "Do not be afraid, Mary; you have found favor with God. You will conceive and give birth to a son, and you are to call him Jesus. He will be great and will be called the Son of the

Do You Know You're Already Amazing?

Most High" (Luke 1:30–32). The difference in the faith of Zechariah and Mary shows up in one simple word. He asks, "How *can* I be sure of this?" and she inquires, "How *will* this be?" (Luke 1:18, 34). Zechariah's encounter with the angel ends in awkward silence. Mary's concludes with her simple declaration: "I am the Lord's servant. . . . May your words to me be fulfilled" (Luke 1:38).

I talked through these two encounters with a wise friend, and she pointed out that Zechariah had seen a lot more of life than Mary. I nodded in understanding and thought back to my own journey with infertility. If an angel had appeared at the beginning to say, "You're going to have a baby!" I would have clapped my hands and gone shopping for a crib. But after almost a decade of enduring that struggle, I admit I might have asked what Zechariah did: "How can I be sure of this?" I think that question is more than just a practical one. It also seems to express, "I've been disappointed too much. Don't get my hopes up."

It's understandable to be self-protecting after all we've endured. It's easy to become a bit cynical. It's tempting to doubt what's outside the realm of our experience. But we serve a God whose ways are mysterious. We never know when he'll show up with wild news, extraordinary plans, and miracles in the making. Even if we are steady, faithful followers, will we be ready to accept his invitation to the impossible—especially farther along in our journeys?

Both Mary and Zechariah received what God foretold, but one waited in silence while the other worshiped with words of praise. Keeping our eyes, minds, and hearts open to what God may do prepares us to respond not as skeptics but as servants. Then we can freely, joyfully declare with Mary, "The Mighty One has done great things for me—holy is his name" (Luke 1:49).

Do You Know You're Already Amazing?

Truth Your Heart Needs

Talk with God about the lies you battle, and ask him to reveal what's true. Listen for his loving voice in your heart, look to his Word, and be honest about what you're feeling.

◆ **What's a Lie I've Battled?** (Example: *I'm not sure God can do what he says.*)

◆ **When or How Did I Begin Battling This Lie?** Ask God to bring a specific memory to mind. If one doesn't come, that's totally okay. Just leave this blank.

◆ **How Do I Need to Be Healed from the Ways This Lie Has Wounded Me?** Write a prayer sharing honestly with God about how this lie has hurt you and asking him to heal your heart.

◆ **What's the Truth That Will Defeat This Lie in My Life?** (Example: *God will do whatever he says.*) Ask God what's really true, and take time to listen for his answer. It may come from today's Scriptures, the devotional, encouraging words from someone in your life, or his still small voice within your heart.

Do You Know You're Already Amazing?

21

You're Blessed with God's Best

"I have to be the best."—Monica

"I am blessed."—Elizabeth, mother of John the Baptist

Read Luke 1:39–45

Monica slams her gym locker and stomps toward the exit, but someone blocks her path. "Whoa," her coach says. "Where are you going so fast? We need to talk." "What's there to talk about?"

responds Monica with a scowl. "I worked longer and harder than anyone else on this team. But you still made Alison the captain." Monica's coach looks her in the eyes and says, "You are a truly talented player. It's not your ability that's holding you back. It's your attitude. You still see every game as being all about you." Monica sighs, then reluctantly admits, "I guess I want to be the best because it makes me feel important." The coach nods in understanding, then puts an arm around Monica's shoulders and walks her out the door. "You're just as important as the captain. But what really matters is that we're a team."

If ancient Israel had a team, then the coveted position young women wanted was to be the mother of the Messiah. Surely if they followed the law, remained pure, and prayed harder than anyone else, then God would pick them. But God's choice surprised everyone. He selected an unmarried, unknown teenager who seemed entirely unqualified in the eyes of the world.

After Mary received the news of God's plan for her life, she went to see her relative Elizabeth. As we talked about in the previous devo-

Do You Know You're Already Amazing?

tional, Elizabeth endured years of infertility, lived righteously, and uttered countless prayers that seemed to go entirely unanswered for so long. It would make sense for her to react to Mary's announcement much like Monica. Yes, she had gotten to be on the team, but clearly someone else had been given the highest honor.

But Elizabeth didn't respond with envy or even question what God had done. Instead, as soon as she saw Mary she said,

> Blessed are you among women, and blessed is the child you will bear! But why am I so favored, that the mother of my Lord should come to me? As soon as the sound of your greeting reached my ears, the baby in my womb leaped for joy. Blessed is she who has believed that the Lord would fulfill his promises to her! (Luke 1:42–45)

Elizabeth's declaration gives us a strategy we can use when the lie "God blesses others more than me" tries to steal our joy.

First, Elizabeth immediately focuses on Mary. She starts with "Blessed are *you*." In the moments when we want to turn inward in self-pity, we can choose to look beyond ourselves instead. God understands this isn't easy, and he can help us see what's happening in the lives of others from a divine perspective rather than our human one.

Then Elizabeth takes an attitude of humility. She asks a question that starts with "why," but not in the way we'd expect. She doesn't ask, "Why didn't God choose me to be the mother of the Messiah instead of this ragtag teenager?" Instead she exclaims, "Why am I so favored, that the mother of my Lord should come to me?" In other words, she's amazed at God's goodness and grateful for the opportunity to be part of it.

Finally, Elizabeth celebrates with Mary and encourages her. I wonder how many times Mary thought back on the words of Elizabeth during hard moments in Jesus' life. (An important note: Sometimes we won't *feel* like celebrating with or encouraging someone else. That's okay—we can just be real, do our best, and trust our emotions will catch up eventually.)

The enemy would like for us to make everything a competition. But God calls us to cooperation. "God has put the body together. . . . If one

Do You Know You're Already Amazing?

part suffers, every part suffers with it; if one part is honored, every part rejoices with it" (1 Cor. 12:24, 26). In other words, when one of us loses, we *all* lose. When one of us wins, we *all* win. We don't have to go through life's victories and defeats alone. And none of us needs to have it all together. We just need to remember we're all better together.

Truth Your Heart Needs

Talk with God about the lies you battle, and ask him to reveal what's true. Listen for his loving voice in your heart, look to his Word, and be honest about what you're feeling.

◆ **What's a Lie I've Battled?** (Example: *I have to be the best.*)

◆ **When or How Did I Begin Battling This Lie?** Ask God to bring a specific memory to mind. If one doesn't come, that's totally okay. Just leave this blank.

◆ **How Do I Need to Be Healed from the Ways This Lie Has Wounded Me?** Write a prayer sharing honestly with God about how this lie has hurt you and asking him to heal your heart.

◆ **What's the Truth That Will Defeat This Lie in My Life?** (Example: *I am blessed.*) Ask God what's really true, and take time to listen for his answer. It may come from today's Scriptures, the devotional, encouraging words from someone in your life, or his still small voice within your heart.

22

Your Future Is Secure

*"My future is in my hands."—widow of
Zarephath before meeting Elijah*

*"My future is in God's hands."—widow of
Zarephath after meeting Elijah*

Read 1 Kings 17:7–24

The hot sun beats down on the back of the widow
from Zarephath (let's call her "Zare" to make it a
bit simpler). She bends to gather another stick
from the ground. Hunger makes her dizzy, and

she hums an old song from her childhood. It's a lamentation—a musical poem of mourning. She thinks of her husband who died far too soon. She thinks of her son back at home wasting away day by day from lack of food. She thinks of herself and how she feels as hollow as the empty flour and oil jars in her barren kitchen. "There is nothing left," she whispers to the wind.

Suddenly, she catches a glimpse of a figure approaching in the distance. Is she seeing a mirage? Has she finally lost her mind? But soon a man is standing in front of her. He has a request: "'Would you bring me a little water in a jar so I may have a drink?' As she was going to get it, he called, 'And bring me, please, a piece of bread'" (1 Kings 17:10–11). Zare laughs to herself and thinks, "He has no idea what he's asking."

For a moment she thinks of pretending she's fine, but something in his steady gaze draws out the truth. "'As surely as the LORD your God lives,' she replied, 'I don't have any bread—only a handful of flour in a jar and a little olive oil in a jug. I am gathering a few sticks to take home and make a meal for myself and my son, that we may eat it—and die'" (1 Kings 17:12). The man, who is the prophet Elijah, responds with compassion and a challenge.

> Don't be afraid. Go home and do as you have said. But first make a small loaf of bread for me from what you have and bring it to me, and then make something for yourself and your son. For this is what the LORD, the God of Israel, says: "The jar of flour will not be used up and the jug of oil will not run dry until the day the LORD sends rain on the land." (1 Kings 17:13–14)

This is Zare's moment of decision. Her turning point. The fork in the road where she can decide to control her future or release it. Obedience could mean a miracle. But if this prophet or his God don't come through, then she's lost all she has. While our circumstances may not be as dramatic, we all find ourselves in a similar place at times. We may not have much, but it's *ours*. Then God comes along and says, "Give me everything. Yes, even that little bit you've been holding back just in case you need it." Our "flour" and "oil" might be money, accomplishments, our reputation, the approval of others—whatever we see as our security.

Zare put her last hopes on the line when she "went away and did as Elijah had told her" (1 Kings 17:15). And God fulfills what he promised through the prophet. "So there was food every day for Elijah and for the woman and her family. For the jar of flour was not used up and the jug of oil did not run dry, in keeping with the word of the LORD spoken by Elijah" (1 Kings 17:15–16).

Zare must have been overjoyed. But she faces one more tragedy before becoming fully convinced her future is in God's hands.

Besides daily food, having a son meant security for a widow because she would be taken care of in her old age. But as time goes by, Zare's son becomes ill. When he dies, she immediately seeks out Elijah. The prophet fervently asks God to bring her son back to life, and his prayer is answered with another miracle. Only then does Zare finally say, "Now I know that you are a man of God and that the word of the LORD from your mouth is the truth" (1 Kings 17:24).

Scripture is silent about the rest of Zare's story. Perhaps she spent her remaining days in peace. Perhaps she encountered more difficulties. Whatever life brought, she now knew she would ultimately be okay. Not because she had food and a son. But because she had come to a point of truly believing in God and his care for her.

We don't have a guarantee hard things won't happen in our lives. We aren't promised we will get what we want. God doesn't always supernaturally intervene like he did with Zare. But no matter what happens, we can know he sees our needs, cares about our hurts, and will provide for us.

We can trust him with today. And tomorrow too.

Do You Know You're Already Amazing?

Truth Your Heart Needs

Talk with God about the lies you battle, and ask him to reveal what's true. Listen for his loving voice in your heart, look to his Word, and be honest about what you're feeling.

◆ **What's a Lie I've Battled?** (Example: *My future is in my hands.*)

◆ **When or How Did I Begin Battling This Lie?** Ask God to bring a specific memory to mind. If one doesn't come, that's totally okay. Just leave this blank.

◆ **How Do I Need to Be Healed from the Ways This Lie Has Wounded Me?** Write a prayer sharing honestly with God about how this lie has hurt you and asking him to heal your heart.

◆ **What's the Truth That Will Defeat This Lie in My Life?** (Example: *My future is in God's hands.*) Ask God what's really true, and take time to listen for his answer. It may come from today's Scriptures, the devotional, encouraging words from someone in your life, or his still small voice within your heart.

Do You Know You're Already Amazing?

23

You Can Be a Mother in Many Ways

"I'm only a mother through physical children."—Amanda

"God makes women mothers in many ways."—Deborah

Read Judges 4–5

A single pink line appears on yet another pregnancy test. Amanda buries her head in her hands and whispers, "When are you going to make me a mother, Lord?" It seems everyone she knows is rocking babies, pushing strollers, and welcoming second, third, even fourth children while she still waits for her first. When she's with her friends, she feels like she doesn't quite fit—as if she's somehow less of a woman without a child of her own.

I've shared how I faced a similar struggle to Amanda. A turning point came in my journey as I read the third chapter of Genesis one morning. In it Eve is called "the mother of all the living" (Gen. 3:20). In that moment God seemed to whisper this truth to my heart: *All women are mothers, because all women bring life to the world in some way.*

We encourage. We feed bellies and hearts. We nurture dreams. We create beauty. We birth books. And yes, some of us also have physical children. But that's not the only way to bring life into this world—it's one of many. Deborah, a judge in ancient Israel, would agree. In a time when women were not usually given leadership positions, she found herself in a place of influence. Those around her looked to her for wisdom.

Do You Know You're Already Amazing?

She also served as a mighty warrior who helped win a significant victory on God's behalf. She said, "Villagers in Israel would not fight; they held back until I, Deborah, arose, until I arose, *a mother in Israel*" (Judg. 5:7).

Scripture gives no indication that Deborah had children of her own. Yet she clearly saw herself as a strong, fierce mama. Because of her courage and obedience, "The land had peace for forty years" (Judg. 5:31).

I believe every woman is tempted at some point to believe she's not a mother. Perhaps you've never married and wonder if you're disqualified from mothering. Maybe you have children but feel inadequate and like you're "not really a mother" compared to others. You might be an empty nester who believes your work as a mom ended when your children left home. You could have dealt with challenges, mistakes, or tragedies that make it seem like you've lost your chance. Whatever your circumstances, I want to gently challenge you to believe this: *you are a mother*.

God may have you mother your department at work, a group of giggling teenagers at church, or the children running wild in your neighborhood. He might have you mentor individuals who never got what they needed from their own moms to truly thrive. He could have you give birth to a project, idea, or dream that wouldn't make it into this world without you.

A beautiful quote by Jill Churchill says, "There's no way to be a perfect mother but a million ways to be a good one."[1] You might be a warrior-mother like Deborah who fights battles to protect the helpless. You might be a gentle, quiet mother who knows how to bring peace to sleepy babies and weary hearts. You might be a mother of many. You might be a mother to one. You might be a mother who spends much of her time at home. You might be a mother who travels the world and has "children" all over the globe.

And while your biological clock may wind down, God's desire to make the most of the time he's given you never stops. Some of the most powerful examples of mothering in Scripture take place long after the natural age for bearing children. If you are still on this earth, then there is someone or something you can mother.

Do You Know You're Already Amazing?

How God calls each of us to mother looks different and may even vary throughout the stages of our lives. But what we all have in common is this: we are a powerful force God wants to use to change the world. Never underestimate what God can do through the heart and hands of a woman. We are influencers. We are nurturers. We are fighters. We are Deborahs. *We are mothers*.

We don't need lines on a pregnancy test as proof. The God-written lines of our life stories already show it's true.

Truth Your Heart Needs

Talk with God about the lies you battle, and ask him to reveal what's true. Listen for his loving voice in your heart, look to his Word, and be honest about what you're feeling.

◆ **What's a Lie I've Battled?** (Example: *I'm only a mother through physical children.*)

◆ **When or How Did I Begin Battling This Lie?** Ask God to bring a specific memory to mind. If one doesn't come, that's totally okay. Just leave this blank.

Do You Know You're Already Amazing?

◆ **How Do I Need to Be Healed from the Ways This Lie Has Wounded Me?** Write a prayer sharing honestly with God about how this lie has hurt you and asking him to heal your heart.

◆ **What's the Truth That Will Defeat This Lie in My Life?** (Example: *God makes women mothers in many ways.*) Ask God what's really true, and take time to listen for his answer. It may come from today's Scriptures, the devotional, encouraging words from someone in your life, or his still small voice within your heart.

24

You Really Are Forgiven

"I've sinned too much for Jesus to forgive me."—Samantha

"I love so much because Jesus has forgiven me."—sinful woman who anointed Jesus

Read Luke 7:36–50

Samantha slides into the last pew of the country church on the edge of town. She used to come here as a child, but it's been years since she dared cross the threshold. The light streaming through the windows makes her hangover headache pound. She pulls her shades from the pocket of the skirt she snatched off the floor of a stranger's bedroom this morning. She knows she probably shouldn't wear sunglasses here, but it's just too much. Everything is so bright. So polished. So clean. Except her.

The preacher's voice booms from the pulpit, "God sees and knows everything you do! You can't fool him!" Samantha sinks lower in her chair. The heads in front of her nod in righteous unison. When the congregation closes their eyes to pray, she sneaks out the back. The door slams louder than she intended, along with her last hopes of ever being forgiven.

Centuries before, another sinful woman made her way to a religious place as well. In her hands she carried an expensive jar of perfume made from alabaster (so let's nickname her "Ali"). She knows she won't be welcome in the home of the Pharisee where Jesus is having dinner. But she's not going to let that stop her. She's already built up a tolerance to shame. Ali manages to enter unnoticed and finds the one she seeks. "As she stood behind him at his feet weeping, she began to wet his feet with her tears. Then she wiped them with her hair, kissed them and poured perfume on them" (Luke 7:38).

She's making a spectacle of herself. She's being a bother. She's doing everything wrong. A woman at a dinner party for men. A sinner touching someone holy. An uninvited guest stealing the show. But all that matters to her is that Jesus knows, sees, hears, feels, understands how sorry she is for all the other, greater wrongs that have come before. Repentant tears replace her voice, but she listens as the men begin to discuss her presence. She waits for the rebuke. And one comes, but to her amazement, it's not directed toward her. Jesus speaks:

> Do you see this woman? I came into your house. You did not give me any water for my feet, but she wet my feet with her tears and wiped them with her hair. You did not give me a kiss, but this woman, from the time I entered, has not stopped kissing my feet. You did not put oil on my head, but she has poured perfume on my feet.

Do You Know You're Already Amazing?

Therefore, I tell you, her many sins have been forgiven—as her great love has shown. But whoever has been forgiven little loves little. (Luke 7:44–47)

Forgiven. The word explodes in Ali's heart like a burst of light. She weeps even more, but now her tears are ones of joy. She pours out the last drops of precious perfume. It's worth about a year's wages. Quite likely it was her dowry—her hopes for the future. Certainly it is one of the only pure things in her life. And she has given it all to the One who has given her what she needed most. Her Savior looks at her with tenderness and says, "Your faith has saved you; go in peace" (Luke 7:50).

Ali leaves with her head held high. For the first time in years, she dares to meet the eyes of others in the street. She wears a wide grin that prompts questions from those who are familiar with her empty expression. She tells her story of sin, mistakes, and amazing grace. By the time she reaches home, she's filled with wonder and anticipation. From now on everything will be different. Because *she* is different.

Sometimes we, like Samantha, can experience criticism and rejection in the places where we most long for acceptance. But that is not an accurate reflection of our Savior. We can always approach him as we are. Our sins are not too much for him. Nothing we can ever do is enough to make him turn us away. When we offer him our tears, fears, secrets, and hidden treasures, it is beautiful in his sight. Let's dare to pour out our hearts to him. Dare to discover his scandalous mercy. Dare to simply *come*.

Truth Your Heart Needs

Talk with God about the lies you battle, and ask him to reveal what's true. Listen for his loving voice in your heart, look to his Word, and be honest about what you're feeling.

◆ **What's a Lie I've Battled?** (Example: *I've sinned too much for Jesus to forgive me.*)

◆ **When or How Did I Begin Battling This Lie?** Ask God to bring a specific memory to mind. If one doesn't come, that's totally okay. Just leave this blank.

◆ **How Do I Need to Be Healed from the Ways This Lie Has Wounded Me?** Write a prayer sharing honestly with God about how this lie has hurt you and asking him to heal your heart.

◆ **What's the Truth That Will Defeat This Lie in My Life?** (Example: *I love so much because Jesus has forgiven me.*) Ask God what's really true, and take time to listen for his answer. It may come from today's Scriptures, the devotional, encouraging words from someone in your life, or his still small voice within your heart.

Do You Know You're Already Amazing?

25

You Can Go outside Your Comfort Zone

"I have to stay inside my comfort zone."—Pam

*"I can go wherever God calls me."
—Rebekah*

Read Genesis 24

The email pops into Pam's inbox, and the subject line jumps out at her: "Job Offer." It's the response she's been waiting to receive. Her hand shakes a bit as she clicks to open it. "We would love to have you join our team," she reads, and a smile crosses her face. "But we'll need you to relocate so you can be closer to our home office." Suddenly her elation is replaced by fear. She's lived in the same town her entire life. She learned to ride her bike on the sidewalks of Main Street. She knows exactly where to find her favorite flavor of ice cream at the store. Her parents still welcome her back to her childhood home every Sunday evening.

Yet over the last few months she's felt a growing sense that it's time to stretch her wings. Numerous friends and even her family have encouraged her to do so. And when she's prayed about the future, she's sensed God leading her in a new direction. She applied for her dream job but never thought she'd get it. Now it's hers for the taking if only she can find the courage to step outside her comfort zone. She takes a deep breath, and before she can think twice about it, she clicks Delete.

Before email brought news to inboxes, it often arrived at the town well. As Rebekah makes her way toward it, she wonders what she'll find out

Do You Know You're Already Amazing?

or who she'll meet today. Her thoughts are interrupted by a polite request from a stranger. "Please give me a little water from your jar" (Gen. 24:17). Her family has taught her to value hospitality, and she quickly gives the man water, then offers to do the same for his camels.

Little does Rebekah know she has just opened the door to an extraordinary adventure. The man is a servant who has been sent to find a wife for his master Abraham's son. The servant has just finished praying, "May it be that when I say to a young woman, 'Please let down your jar that I may have a drink,' and she says, 'Drink, and I'll water your camels too'—let her be the one you have chosen for your servant Isaac. By this I will know that you have shown kindness to my master" (Gen. 24:14).

What follows is a whirlwind. The servant goes to the home of Rebekah's family and shares how God is at work. Then he requests for Rebekah to return with him immediately to become the wife of Isaac. Her family responds, "'Let's call the young woman and ask her about it.' So they called Rebekah and asked her, 'Will you go with this man?'" (Gen. 24:57–58). It's a life-changing moment of decision. Like Pam, Rebekah had spent her whole life in one place. She still lived in her father's home. She likely had never ventured farther than the borders of her town. Yet she replies simply and powerfully, "I will go" (Gen. 24:58). Her brave act of obedience alters the course of her life, lands her in the lineage of the Messiah, and begins a great love story.

When Isaac sees Rebekah, he's smitten at first sight in one of the most romantic passages in Scripture:

> He went out to the field one evening to meditate, and as he looked up, he saw camels approaching. Rebekah also looked up and saw Isaac. . . . Then the servant told Isaac all he had done. Isaac brought her into the tent of his mother Sarah, and he married Rebekah. So she became his wife, and he loved her; and Isaac was comforted after his mother's death. (Gen. 24:63–64, 66–67)

If we always stick to what seems safest and most familiar, we risk missing out on what God has planned for us. Instead we can simply pray,

Do You Know You're Already Amazing?

"God, I'm open to whatever you have for me today. Even if what I face is unknown, I know you. I trust you to take care of me wherever you call me to go." Leaving our comfort zone may mean an actual change in location, like it did for Pam and Rebekah. But it can also happen right where we are each day. It might look like reaching out to others who are different than us. Learning something new. Pursuing a dream. We like to put limits on our lives, but we serve a limitless God who invites us to move beyond what has confined and defined us.

The best place to be is not our comfort zone. It's the center of God's will.

Truth Your Heart Needs

Talk with God about the lies you battle, and ask him to reveal what's true. Listen for his loving voice in your heart, look to his Word, and be honest about what you're feeling.

◆ **What's a Lie I've Battled?** (Example: *I have to stay inside my comfort zone.*)

◆ **When or How Did I Begin Battling This Lie?** Ask God to bring a specific memory to mind. If one doesn't come, that's totally okay. Just leave this blank.

Do You Know You're Already Amazing?

◆ **How Do I Need to Be Healed from the Ways This Lie Has Wounded Me?** Write a prayer sharing honestly with God about how this lie has hurt you and asking him to heal your heart.

◆ **What's the Truth That Will Defeat This Lie in My Life?** (Example: *I can go wherever God calls me.*) Ask God what's really true, and take time to listen for his answer. It may come from today's Scriptures, the devotional, encouraging words from someone in your life, or his still small voice within your heart.

26

You Can Let Go
without Giving Up

"I have no choice but to give up."
—Hebrew slave women

"I can choose to give this to God."
—Jochebed, mother of Moses

Read Exodus 1:15–2:10; Numbers 26:59

Jochebed's dread grew each day along with her belly. It wouldn't be long until her child made an appearance. One question filled her thoughts from morning until night: Would she have a boy or girl? The Egyptian Pharaoh had become concerned about the growing population of Hebrew slaves. He came up with a simple, heartless solution: kill all male children. But the God-fearing midwives rebelled, and for a season the little ones had been safe. "Then the king of Egypt summoned the midwives and asked them, 'Why have you done this? Why have you let the boys live?' The midwives answered Pharaoh, 'Hebrew women are not like Egyptian women; they are vigorous and give birth before the midwives arrive.' So God was kind to the midwives and the people increased and became even more numerous" (Exod. 1:18–20).

Yes, God had been kind, but Pharaoh would never be, and over time he grew weary of the midwives' excuses. So he ordered the Hebrew people to take matters into their own hands. "Then Pharaoh gave this order to all his people: 'Every Hebrew boy that is born you must throw into the Nile, but let every girl live'" (Exod. 1:22). A shudder swept over Jochebed, and she broke out in a cold sweat. Then a familiar, searing pain began to tear at her body. Her little girl, Miriam, appeared at her side with a question in her eyes. "Go tell your daddy it's time," she managed to say before a groan consumed her voice.

Hours later, Amram wiped the blood from his newly born son and tried to calm him. "Shh, shh," he whispered to the infant. "We can't let anyone hear you." This should have been a joyful, triumphant moment for a Hebrew father, but Amram couldn't even look into the baby's eyes. He felt his chest tightening and passed the tiny bundle to his wife. Jochebed felt the weight. What would they do now? She drifted off to sleep as little Moses nursed for the first time. She'd been told to take him to the river immediately—it would be easier that way—but how could she deny her son this bit of comfort?

When she woke, she sensed a whisper within her heart: *"Don't let go."* Although Jochebed had never considered herself a courageous woman, she listened. For three months she hid her ordinary, extraordinary child. Yet the day came when Jochebed knew she could no longer keep her secret. If Moses was discovered, he would immediately

Do You Know You're Already Amazing?

be killed. The rest of her family would likely suffer the same fate. Over and over again she'd clung to the same inner instruction. But now there seemed to be a change she didn't understand.

Tears streamed down Jochebed's face as she placed Moses in a basket woven from papyrus. "I feel like I'm giving up," she prayed with a broken heart as she walked to the Nile. *You're not giving up*, the Lord seemed to reassure her. *You're giving him to me.* She nestled her son's tiny carrier in the reeds along the riverbank and stepped back. Overcome with emotion, she instructed Miriam, "Stay here and watch your brother." Miriam nodded, and soon a group of women in fancy clothes approached the water.

> Then Pharaoh's daughter went down to the Nile to bathe, and her attendants were walking along the riverbank. She saw the basket among the reeds and sent her female slave to get it. She opened it and saw the baby. He was crying, and she felt sorry for him. "This is one of the Hebrew babies," she said.
>
> Then his sister asked Pharaoh's daughter, "Shall I go and get one of the Hebrew women to nurse the baby for you?"

"Yes, go," she answered. So the girl went and got the baby's mother. (Exod. 2:5–8)

Jochebed joyfully raced back to the river to hold the child she had surrendered not long before. She smelled his sweet, familiar skin as he instantly relaxed in her arms. And as she nursed him without fear for the first time, her whole being exclaimed, "Thank you, God!"

We will all have a "Moses" moment at some point in our lives. Perhaps it will involve a person we love but must release, a desire we need to surrender, or a dream we're being asked to lay down. Yes, there is a time to hold on with all our hearts. But there is also a perfect, God-appointed time to let go. When we obey that still, small prompting, we're not giving up—we're giving our mighty, wise God the opportunity to do what only he can.

Do You Know You're Already Amazing?

Truth Your Heart Needs

Talk with God about the lies you battle, and ask him to reveal what's true. Listen for his loving voice in your heart, look to his Word, and be honest about what you're feeling.

◆ **What's a Lie I've Battled?** (Example: *I have no choice but to give up.*)

◆ **When or How Did I Begin Battling This Lie?** Ask God to bring a specific memory to mind. If one doesn't come, that's totally okay. Just leave this blank.

◆ **How Do I Need to Be Healed from the Ways This Lie Has Wounded Me?** Write a prayer sharing honestly with God about how this lie has hurt you and asking him to heal your heart.

◆ **What's the Truth That Will Defeat This Lie in My Life?** (Example: *I can choose to give this to God.*) Ask God what's really true, and take time to listen for his answer. It may come from today's Scriptures, the devotional, encouraging words from someone in your life, or his still small voice within your heart.

Do You Know You're Already Amazing?

27

You're Created to Give God Glory

"I need the recognition and admiration."
– Miriam in the desert

"I need to give God glory and praise."
—Miriam when God delivered the Israelites

Read Exodus 15:1–21

Miriam thought back to the day her baby brother was pulled from the Nile by an Egyptian princess. Was that when the seed of envy began quietly growing in her heart? She watched as Moses got all the best this life could offer—a beautiful palace to live in, the finest foods to eat, the respect that comes with royalty—while she grew up to be a slave just like the rest of her family.

One day she overheard a fellow Hebrew saying Moses had killed an Egyptian taskmaster for mistreating one of their people. Not long after that, her brother vanished completely. She missed him, but perhaps some part of her also felt relief to no longer hear "Moses this, Moses that" from the lips of her parents. God had delivered him from destruction as a baby, and they hoped their son would return the favor by doing the same for their people. But it seemed Moses had let fear decide his fate.

Years later a neighbor burst into her home with astounding news to share. Moses was back! Along with her brother Aaron, he appeared before Pharaoh and demanded the freedom of the Hebrews. Soon Moses and Aaron sought Miriam out. They talked for hours about what God was doing. Soon one terrible plague followed another as the leader of Egypt refused to obey the divine instruction to let the Hebrews go. But finally, in the middle of the night, an urgent knock came at her door. Already awake, Miriam rushed to answer and was told, "It's time." After the sudden death of all the firstborns in Egypt, Pharaoh had finally relented.

The streets were filled with shouts of joy, and tears freely flowed as the Hebrew people prepared to leave. Miriam took her place at the front along with her brothers. She looked in awe at God's presence in front of them. It would appear as a cloud by day and pillar of fire by night to guide them on their journey to the Promised Land. But the celebration didn't last. Once Pharaoh overcame his initial grief, his hardened heart became unrepentant again. He pursued the Israelites.

Miriam heard the thunder of chariots behind them and looked at the waves in front of them. What would they do now? Then Moses lifted his arms and the Red Sea parted. They walked across on dry ground. When the Egyptian army tried to do the same, the water covered them completely. If Miriam ever had doubts, they were washed away as well. She "took a timbrel in her hand, and all the women followed her, with timbrels and dancing. Miriam sang to them: 'Sing to the LORD, for he is highly exalted. Both horse and driver he has hurled into the sea'" (Exod. 15:20–21). Miriam felt completely consumed by a desire to bring glory and praise to God.

But after years in the desert, Miriam's timbrel had almost turned to dust. The praises she once sang had grown silent too. Instead she grumbled with her brother Aaron. "'Has the LORD spoken only through Moses?' they asked. 'Hasn't he also spoken through us?'" (Num. 12:2). It was her childhood all over again. Moses gets the attention. Moses gets the admiration. Moses gets the credit. Sometimes she wished she'd pushed his papyrus basket down the river. Every day the bitterness inside her had silently grown until it threatened to consume her.

Miriam and Aaron's complaining session got cut short when they were divinely summoned, along with Moses, to the tent of meeting. God spoke of Moses' faithfulness and friendship, then asked his siblings why they dared to speak

Do You Know You're Already Amazing?

against him. When the cloud of God's presence lifted, Miriam was covered with leprosy, a serious disease that leads to a slow, painful death. She was too startled to even speak, but Aaron instantly begged Moses to intercede for his sister. God granted Moses' request with one condition—Miriam must spend seven days alone outside the camp.

God's actions may seem harsh, but I believe there is mysterious mercy in them. He allowed Miriam to see with her eyes what had been slowly festering in her heart. He knew she needed a clear intervention and time away from everyone to heal in more ways than just physically. She was sick with arrogance, jealousy, and selfishness. Perhaps in the quiet moments she spent outside the camp, God's words about Moses echoed in her ears and she finally understood that what God wanted most from her wasn't a performance. It was a personal relationship.

Miriam once stood on a riverbank and watched God deliver her brother. She'd stood on the shore of a sea and watched God deliver her people. Finally she stood on the edge of an oasis of grace where God wanted to deliver her as well. We're all a bit like Miriam—paradoxes of pride and praise, insecurity and boldness, envy and encouragement. Thankfully, God still reveals, then heals, sin-sick hearts and restores all those who look to him for help. He won't leave us where we are or as we are. He loves us far too much to do so.

Do You Know You're Already Amazing?

Truth Your Heart Needs

Talk with God about the lies you battle, and ask him to reveal what's true. Listen for his loving voice in your heart, look to his Word, and be honest about what you're feeling.

◆ **What's a Lie I've Battled?** (Example: *I need recognition and admiration.*)

◆ **When or How Did I Begin Battling This Lie?** Ask God to bring a specific memory to mind. If one doesn't come, that's totally okay. Just leave this blank.

◆ **How Do I Need to Be Healed from the Ways This Lie Has Wounded Me?** Write a prayer sharing honestly with God about how this lie has hurt you and asking him to heal your heart.

◆ **What's the Truth That Will Defeat This Lie in My Life?** (Example: *I need to give God the glory and praise.*) Ask God what's really true, and take time to listen for his answer. It may come from today's Scriptures, the devotional, encouraging words from someone in your life, or his still small voice within your heart.

Do You Know You're Already Amazing?

28

You're Not in Control

"If I do what's right, nothing will go wrong."—Jane

"When something goes wrong, God can make it right."—Tabitha

Read Acts 9:36–42

The doctor comes into the room with a grim look on her face. "The biopsy results are back. You have cancer. We'll need to start aggressive treatments immediately." Jane protests, "But I ate well. I exercised. I've never smoked. This isn't supposed to happen to me." Her physician gives her a look of sympathy and says, "Not everything is under our control."

As Jane drives home, her thoughts turn to a different path. If a physical choice didn't cause her cancer, then maybe a spiritual one did. She's messed up somehow and God is punishing her. Starting right now she'll pray harder, read her Bible more, and make sure she's loving toward everyone she meets. Then surely God will heal her. Jane sighs with relief at first, but underneath her new plan, the old fear remains.

Tabitha sighs too as she adds the final touches to the simple dress she's been making. But the sound she makes is one of contentment. This afternoon she'll carry clothing to the widows and orphans in her town along with the bread she can smell baking in the oven. When she stands, she feels a bit light-headed and thinks, "Maybe I'll just rest for a bit before I go."

Hours later she's awakened by a knock at the door. "Tabitha? Are you there?" She recognizes the voice of a young widow she frequently visits. She hears footsteps coming toward her

Do You Know You're Already Amazing?

room. "You didn't show up this afternoon and I was worried," the girl says. She raises a hand to Tabitha's forehead and a look of alarm fills her eyes. "I'm going to get a doctor." But somehow Tabitha knows a doctor won't be able to bring her back from the journey she's already begun. She quietly repeats her favorite psalm: "Though I walk through the valley of the shadow of death, I will fear no evil; For You *are* with me; Your rod and Your staff, they comfort me" (Ps. 23:4 NKJV).

The next thing her earthly ears hear is Peter's voice commanding, "Tabitha, get up" (Acts 9:40). At first she's confused by the tear-streaked faces surrounding her. She feels better than ever. Why are they so worried? But slowly she realizes that what she just experienced wasn't a dream. She left this world, and then Jesus brought her back again. She looks at the pile of fabric still sitting on the table and the cooled bread beside it. Everyone laughs with relief as she declares, "I'm not finished yet!"

Tucked away in the story of Tabitha is a truth we all need to know. *Even if we do everything right, things can still go wrong.* Like many people today, the ancient Jews believed life's troubles were always a result of disobedience. Even the disciples had to learn this wasn't true. When they saw a man blind from birth, "[Jesus'] disciples asked him, 'Rabbi, who sinned, this man or his parents, that he was born blind?' 'Neither this man nor his parents sinned,' said Jesus, 'but this happened so that the works of God might be displayed in him'" (John 9:2–3).

In his mysterious ways, God allows certain hardships in order to fulfill his purposes. We also experience pain and loss simply because we live in a fallen, broken world where things are not as they should be. Either way, we can't completely avoid difficulties. In other words, *we're not in control*. While this is frustrating to hear at first, ultimately it can be freeing. Because if we're not in control, that means we don't have to live like everything depends on us. We don't have to make sure we're perfect so we won't get punished. We don't have to be afraid we won't be able to handle what happens. We don't have to work hard to keep God happy so we get what we want and the blessings keep coming.

Sometimes life's greatest gifts may even come from the hardest, most unexpected places. That's possible because "in all things God works for the good of those who love him, who have been called according to his purpose" (Rom. 8:28). Those words are not a hollow cliché. They're not a shallow way to comfort someone when we don't know what to say. They're a promise. They're our hope. They're the reason we can say, "God, I don't understand, but I'm still placing my life in your hands today."

Truth Your Heart Needs

Talk with God about the lies you battle, and ask him to reveal what's true. Listen for his loving voice in your heart, look to his Word, and be honest about what you're feeling.

◆ **What's a Lie I've Battled?** (Example: *If I do what's right, nothing will go wrong.*)

◆ **When or How Did I Begin Battling This Lie?** Ask God to bring a specific memory to mind. If one doesn't come, that's totally okay. Just leave this blank.

Do You Know You're Already Amazing?

◆ **How Do I Need to Be Healed from the Ways This Lie Has Wounded Me?** Write a prayer sharing honestly with God about how this lie has hurt you and asking him to heal your heart.

◆ **What's the Truth That Will Defeat This Lie in My Life?** (Example: *When something goes wrong, God can make it right.*) Ask God what's really true, and take time to listen for his answer. It may come from today's Scriptures, the devotional, encouraging words from someone in your life, or his still small voice within your heart.

29

You're Not Condemned

"I am condemned."—woman caught in adultery, before meeting Jesus

"I am no longer condemned."—woman caught in adultery, after meeting Jesus

Read John 8:1–11

She clutches a thin robe around her and stumbles through the street with the harsh hand of a Pharisee on her elbow. She tries to resist, but he only gives her a stern look and pushes her forward. His dismissive expression says, "You're only an object to be used." She's seen that look in the eyes of men ever since her childhood. She thought this last one would be different, but then she'd been caught right in the middle of the act of adultery. The Pharisees knew where to find the two of them. Yet she's the only one being paraded through town. It certainly seems her lover has betrayed her. At the very least, he's failed to protect her like he promised.

The group reaches the temple courts, and as they enter she can hear the gentle voice of a young man teaching. "There he is," says one Pharisee. "We'll see if Jesus can get out of this one." Suddenly she knows why she's there—as bait to catch the said-to-be Messiah. "They made her stand before the group and said to Jesus, 'Teacher, this woman was caught in the act of adultery. In the Law Moses commanded us to stone such women. Now what do you say?' They were using this question as a trap, in order to have a basis for accusing him" (John 8:3–6). Her heart begins to pound with fear. Stone her? She can already see one of the men picking up rocks.

She's horrified as he begins to place one in each hand of those surrounding her.

As if the situation isn't urgent, Jesus bends and slowly begins to write in the sand. The religious men continue to hurl questions at him like warm-ups for what they're about to do. Jesus pays no attention. "Say something! Do something!" she wants to scream. Yet she also knows this for certain: she's guilty. Her condemnation is justified. Everything her accusers have said is true. She freely chose to violate God's law. And this isn't the first time. It's simply the only time she's been caught. She swallows hard and thinks, *Maybe if I get the punishment I deserve, then God will forgive me*. She closes her eyes and braces herself for the first blow. Will she die quickly? Or will it be slow and painful? As she stands there, she thinks back over her life. She wishes she could make different choices, but it's too late now.

Finally Jesus speaks. "Let any one of you who is without sin be the first to throw a stone at her" (Luke 8:7). She senses the discomfort sweeping through the crowd. Jesus leans over again and continues scribbling in the dirt. Later there will be speculation that he listed the sins of the Pharisees standing there with rocks in their hands. The first "thud" terrifies her before she realizes it's not a stone being thrown but rather one being dropped. The oldest man in the group turns and walks away. Another follows him. Finally even the youngest has gone. Jesus straightens up and asks her, "Woman, where are they? Has no one condemned you?" (John 8:10). Her voice trembles as she answers, "No one, sir." Then he speaks the words she thought she'd never hear: "'Then neither do I condemn you,' Jesus declared. 'Go now and leave your life of sin'" (John 8:11).

She suddenly understands he's saying this not just as a man but as God. Not just as a polite pat on the head for a wayward child but as a life-changing promise. Not just as an instruction about behavior but as an invitation to an intimate relationship beyond anything she's ever known. A smile sweeps across her face, and she feels the weight of her sin lifted. How had she not realized she had been carrying stones inside her heart too? She condemned herself long before anyone else did. But now she has a second chance. And she's not going to waste it.

We all could be the woman caught in adultery. Perhaps we haven't committed that particular sin, but God sees all we do, and each of us has reason to be accused and condemned. And we could all be the Pharisees. We can wound each other *and our own hearts* with words of condemnation until we're broken and bleeding. But "if anyone does sin, we have Jesus Christ, who has God's full approval. He speaks on our behalf" (1 John 2:1 GW). And "there is now no condemnation for those who are in Christ Jesus" (Rom. 8:1). Jesus speaks only words of love to and for us. That means we're to do the same for each other—*and ourselves too.*

It's time to set down our stones and take hold of grace like our lives depend on it. Because they do.

Do You Know You're Already Amazing?

Truth Your Heart Needs

Talk with God about the lies you battle, and ask him to reveal what's true. Listen for his loving voice in your heart, look to his Word, and be honest about what you're feeling.

◆ **What's a Lie I've Battled?** (Example: *I am condemned.*)

◆ **When or How Did I Begin Battling This Lie?** Ask God to bring a specific memory to mind. If one doesn't come, that's totally okay. Just leave this blank.

◆ **How Do I Need to Be Healed from the Ways This Lie Has Wounded Me?** Write a prayer sharing honestly with God about how this lie has hurt you and asking him to heal your heart.

◆ **What's the Truth That Will Defeat This Lie in My Life?** (Example: *I am no longer condemned.*) Ask God what's really true, and take time to listen for his answer. It may come from today's Scriptures, the devotional, encouraging words from someone in your life, or his still small voice within your heart.

Do You Know You're Already Amazing?

30

You're Already Amazing

"I'm just a mess."—Us

"You are my masterpiece."—God

Read Genesis 1:31; Psalm 139:13–18;
2 Corinthians 5:17; Ephesians 2:10

I recently returned to the place online where I asked the question, "What lies are women tempted to believe about who we are?" As I scrolled back through the answers, I saw all over again how many expressed, "I'm just a mess." In other words, *I can't possibly be amazing.* And yes, none of us are perfect. We "all have sinned and fall short of the glory of God" (Rom. 3:23). But as we've discovered together, that is only part of our story—and Jesus has already rewritten it.

Even some of the first lines about who we are tell a different tale. After we were created, "God looked over all he had made, and he saw that it was very good" (Gen. 1:31 NLT)! The truth is, we are living, walking miracles. There are over ten billion unique cells in our bodies. Our hearts beat more than 100,000 times a day, pumping blood through about 80,000 miles of blood vessels.[1] As David declared:

> You made my whole being;
> > you formed me in my mother's body.
> I praise you because you made me in an
> > amazing and wonderful way.
> > What you have done is wonderful.
> > I know this very well.
> You saw my bones being formed
> > as I took shape in my mother's body.
> When I was put together there,
> you saw my body as it was formed.
> > Psalm 139:13–16 NCV

Do You Know You're Already Amazing?

As if our bodies weren't extraordinary enough, we also reflect the image of God through the unseen, eternal parts of who we are. We are beings with souls. We have hearts full of hopes and desires. God has placed invisible gifts within each of us. And when we give ourselves to Jesus, we are mysteriously created all over again. "If anyone is in Christ, the new creation has come: The old has gone, the new is here!" (2 Cor. 5:17). We are not a factory-assembled product. "We are God's masterpiece" (Eph. 2:10 NLT).

I once helped facilitate a creative retreat for a group of women. I shared encouragement, and other instructors guided the group in art journaling as a response. Here's what I learned: *those journals were messy, but they were not a mess.* They were full of wild loveliness, vivid declarations, and passionate displays of hearts laid open. In many ways, we are God's art journal. We are the expression of his love on history's pages. Is it a neat, practical process? Absolutely not. Just think back over the biblical women we've studied together. So many struggles. So much pain. But also so much strength. So much beauty.

The women at the retreat often offered disclaimers. "It's not really what I want it to be," they'd say. "Hers is better than mine," they'd protest. Some of that came from insecurity, but it also seemed to stem from a fear of being prideful. Don't we do the same? Thankfully, as we just read, David took care of that concern: "I praise you because you made me in an amazing and wonderful way" (Ps. 139:14 NCV). As I've said before, recognizing what's true about who we are leads to *praise*, not to pride.

I chose the word *amazing* for this book because the definition is "causing great wonder."[2] *It's the response our souls have to the creations of an astonishing artist.* My prayer is that seeing the truth about who we are and who God is fills us with new wonder and worship.

As long as we are in this world, we will encounter lies. They will try to erase our faith and cover our identities. But we have this promise: "God, who began a good work within you, will continue his work until it is finally finished on the day when Christ Jesus returns" (Phil. 1:6 NLT).

Do You Know You're Already Amazing?

This is the beautiful paradox we live in as women: Yes, as we talked about in the very beginning, we are warriors. But we are also works of art.

And a work of art in the hands of its Creator doesn't strive; it receives. It yields to the process not of doing but of becoming. It lets itself be filled with a glory not its own.

Dear Maker of All We Are, make that true of us. Amen.

Truth Your Heart Needs

Talk with God about the lies you battle, and ask him to reveal what's true. Listen for his loving voice in your heart, look to his Word, and be honest about what you're feeling.

◆ **What's a Lie I've Battled?** (Example: *I'm just a mess.*)

◆ **When or How Did I Begin Battling This Lie?** Ask God to bring a specific memory to mind. If one doesn't come, that's totally okay. Just leave this blank.

Do You Know You're Already Amazing?

◆ **How Do I Need to Be Healed from the Ways This Lie Has Wounded Me?** Write a prayer sharing honestly with God about how this lie has hurt you and asking him to heal your heart.

◆ **What's the Truth That Will Defeat This Lie in My Life?** (Example: *I'm God's masterpiece.*) Ask God what's really true, and take time to listen for his answer. It may come from today's Scriptures, the devotional, encouraging words from someone in your life, or his still small voice within your heart.

Acknowledgments

As I've written this devotional, so many women who have poured truth into me throughout my life have come to mind. If I mentioned them all, I would need to write another book!

I'm especially grateful for the legacy of faith I've been given by my family and the examples of godly women like my mom, Lynda, and my grandma, Eula.

I'm also thankful for local friends who speak words my heart needs to hear over coffee. And for those far away who send encouragement to my phone and inbox.

And I'm so glad to work with a wonderful group of women at Revell, including Jennifer Leep, Twila Bennett, Wendy Wetzel, and Claudia Marsh. You add so much to my life and words.

For my readers—I appreciate you sharing the journey of *You're Already Amazing* with me. You teach me so much.

Most of all, I praise the God who made me and who gives me the privilege of listening to his heart and then sharing what I hear. He's beyond amazing.

Notes

Chapter 3 You Don't Need to Do It All

1. Joanna Weaver, *Having a Mary Heart in a Martha World: Finding Intimacy with God in the Busyness of Life* (New York: Crown Publishing Group, 2001), 8.

Chapter 4 You're Not Defined by a Man

1. Beth Moore, *So Long, Insecurity: You've Been a Bad Friend to Us* (Carol Stream, IL: Tyndale, 2010), 221.

Chapter 5 Your Life Has a Purpose

1. Brother Lawrence, *The Practice of the Presence of God*, trans. Edgar G. Barton (London: Epworth), in "Fourth Conversation," http://www.ccel.org/ccel/lawrence/practice.iii.iv.html.

Chapter 6 Your Looks Don't Determine Your Worth

1. Ann Spangler and Jean E. Syswerda, *Women of the Bible* (Grand Rapids: Zondervan, 2008), 265–66.

Chapter 16 You Can Trust God's Timing

1. Joanna Weaver, *Lazarus Awakening: Finding Your Place in the Heart of God* (Colorado Springs: Waterbrook, 2012), 81.

2. Quoted in Therese J. Borchard, "Never Place a Period Where God Has Placed a Comma: Why You Need Friends," *Beyond Blue*, Beliefnet.com, http://www.beliefnet.com/columnists/beyondblue/2010/05/never-place-a-period-where-god.html.

Chapter 18 Your Needs and Desires Matter

1. Liz Curtis Higgs, *It's Good to Be Queen: Becoming as Bold, Gracious, and Wise as the Queen of Sheba* (Colorado Springs: Waterbrook, 2015), 17.

Chapter 23 You Can Be a Mother in Many Ways

1. Jill Churchill, *Grime and Punishment* (New York: Avon, 1989), 1.

Chapter 30 You're Already Amazing

1. Dale Stuckwish, "The Human Body Is Fearfully and Wonderfully Made," Examiner.com, January 27, 2013, http://www.examiner.com/article/the-human-body-is-fearfully-and-wonderfully-made.

2. Google definition, s.v. "amazing," https://www.google.com/search?q=definition+of+amazing&ie=utf-8&oe=utf-8.

About Holley

Holley Gerth wishes she could have coffee with you. And if she could, she'd never mention any of this, because she'd be too busy listening to you and loving it.

Holley is the *Wall Street Journal* bestselling author of *You're Already Amazing* as well as several other books. She's also a licensed counselor, certified life coach, and speaker who helps women embrace who they are, become all God created them to be, and live intentionally.

Holley cofounded (in)courage.me, an online destination for women that received almost one million page views in its first six months. She also partners with DaySpring. Her personal site, Holley Gerth.com, serves over 30,000 subscribers.

Outside the word world, Holley is the wife of Mark, and together they're parents to Lovelle—a daughter they adopted when she was twenty-one years old because God is full of surprises.

Until you can have that cup of coffee with her, Holley would love to connect with you in these places:

Blog: www.holleygerth.com
Facebook: Holley Gerth (author page)
Twitter: @HolleyGerth
Instagram: holleygerth
Pinterest: Holley Gerth

"Holley Gerth turns words like a poet. Warm and personal, *You're Already Amazing* is a biblical, practical handbook for every woman's heart."

— Emily P. Freeman, author of *Grace for the Good Girl*

With this heart-to-heart message, Holley Gerth invites you to embrace one very important truth—that you truly are already amazing. Like a trusted friend, Holley gently shows you how to forget the lies and expectations the world feeds you and instead believe that God loves you and has bigger plans for your life than you've ever imagined.

Revell
a division of Baker Publishing Group
www.RevellBooks.com

Available wherever books and ebooks are sold.

More exciting ways to enjoy

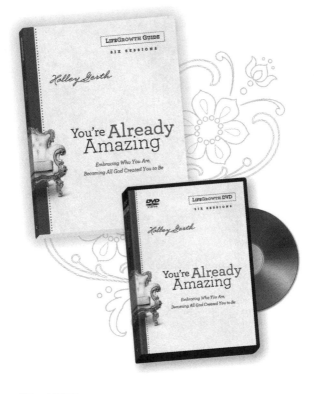

You're Already Amazing!

Grab a friend (or more than one!) and your favorite beverage and gather 'round to learn more about your unique identity as a child of God as well as practical ways to bring change into your relationships and daily lives.

The *You're Already Amazing LifeGrowth Guide* (based on the book *You're Already Amazing*) will lead you through a six-week study with:

- *free videos at HolleyGerth.com/amazing or available on DVD for easy access*

- *questions for groups to discuss or individuals to reflect on*

- *interactive tools based on Holley's training as a counselor and life coach to help you apply what you're reading*

- *optional creative activities you can do with a group or on your own*

- *prompts for personal journaling*

Discover the dreams God has given you—
and then dare to pursue them.

Holley Gerth takes you by the heart and says, "Yes! You can do this!"
She guides you with insightful questions, action plans to take
the next steps, and most of all, the loving hand of a friend.

If your life isn't perfect . . .
If you've ever been disappointed . . .
If you feel stressed or tired . . .
This is for you.

"Holley Gerth is a fresh voice for every woman—
she echoes the voice of our Father."

—Ann Voskamp, *New York Times* bestselling
author of *One Thousand Gifts*